MW00622256

Celestial Shamanism

Using Interstellar Light Codes to Find Your Authentic Path in a Shifting Human Paradigm

Yvonne Perry

Copyright © 2020 by Yvonne Perry

Celestial Shamanism™ ~ Using Interstellar Light Codes to Find Your Authentic Path in a Shifting Human Paradigm

Published and printed in the United States of America.

All rights reserved. Under International Copyright Law, no part of this book may be reproduced, stored, or transmitted by any means–electronic, mechanical, photographic (photocopy), recording, or otherwise–without the written permission from the publisher. *Celestial Shamanism™* is trademarked by Yvonne Perry with the publication of this book and the use of the term on her website and blog.

Cover design by Emily Singleton.
Edited by Dana Michelli

ISBN: 978-0-9890688-3-3
Write On! Publishing
Nashville, Tennessee
September 2020

http:// WeAre1inSpirit.com

All right reserved. No part of this book might be reproduced by any mechanical, photographic, or electronic process, or in the form of a recording; nor may it be stored in a retrieval system, transmitted, or otherwise copied for public or private use other than brief quotations for fair use.

Disclaimer: This book contains the opinions and thoughts of its author and is not intended to provide professional services or medical/psychological advice or for making diagnoses or treatment of any illness. The intent of the author is to offer information to help you in your pursuit of emotional, physical, and spiritual well-being. The publisher/author claims no responsibility or liability for loss or risk incurred as a result of the use or application of any of the contents of the book.

Dedication

To all lightworkers, celestial shamans and their galactic teams. To Mother Earth and Father Sky and all the children of light.

Contents

Foreword

I had returned to Ishatae, the small cabin at Highland Realm, to begin documenting thirty years of my work. Yvonne had recently moved not far from there to begin her new life and to give birth to a book that she felt ready to write. The timing of this seemed to have special meaning, for while we always felt we would "do" something together, we always seemed to move in different directions.

Having met Yvonne many years ago, I had learned to not be surprised by anything our conversations might reveal. Every conversation seemed to bring a new sense of collaboration as we each felt the emergence of a new phase of our individual work that reached beyond what could be done by one person alone. Now, it was finally time to explore our next step.

Yvonne and I are quite different in our work on the planet—mine being technical, with EarthProject777, and hers working with light language and counseling starseeds, walk-ins and others experiencing the dramatic shifts currently occurring on the planet. Yet as we began to catch up in Starbucks that day, we realized that our differences were suddenly finding a new common thread of similarity. The recent planetary shift was a clear indication that we would finally see how our collaboration would assist us both as we moved forward. Filling in the gaps since our last meeting, Yvonne told me about her new book concept, one that fit closely with an anomaly revealed during my own work. The deeper we moved into the conversation the clearer our pathway became. She asked if she could interview me for her new book, as some of my technical information gave validation to the information she was receiving. Some hours later, it was obvious that WE had stepped into our new roles and together, WE would weave a tapestry for future generations.

We began by honoring our diverse skillsets, trusting the process and each other and committing to the fullness of our collaboration, letting nothing stand in the way, agreeing to move through any challenges and holding one another accountable. At times, we would have to reset and allow a PAUSE as we searched for ways to better understand what the other was talking about. Even that became easier as we each learned to listen in a new way. Sounds like a challenge . . . instead it has been a gift.

The interview took most of the day as we answered questions, filled in gaps and expanded our individual perceptions to include a deeper understanding of our combined interpretations. This required special care, as our language interpretation differences would need to encompass a third point of synthesis in order for Yvonne to take this new information to those she has come to serve. As the day progressed WE began to bridge the gap between her light language and the directives from EarthProject777; our commitment to the unfolding brought many ah-has and WE knew we were ready. Soon Yvonne began sending me chapters of the new book, and as I read them I found myself awestruck by the understanding and ease with which she gave voice to the concept of shamanism: in the ancient tradition, through the anomalies, and finally into the integrated, embodied concept of Celestial Shamanism™. In the Beginning, the indigenous shaman was one with the Earth, nature, and all that exists. Yvonne takes us through the many changes and models ways in which we might remember this union: by connecting once again with our humanity, the wisdom of the Divine and the rhythm of nature, feeling the whispers as nature guides the way for us to move with Gaia. Yvonne has given us a glimpse of how we might take our "next first step," individually and collectively.

Though this interview may seem like a one-sided exchange, let me assure you that I have benefited from it in many ways, both personally and with regard to giving new voice to my own technical work. I was finally given an opportunity to see the Directives of EarthProject7™, The Tri-Vector SYSTEM™, and RBQT-18"™ come to life in a new way. Yvonne was able to translate the work and use it with her client base, in her own way and opening a pathway for others to do the same. Finally, WE had closed a circle—our individual work had come together in ONE voice.

Whether you are a seasoned explorer into life's mystery or just beginning your journey, I can assure you that the information in this book will expand your experiential vocabulary and give you ways to open conversations with others who might be having similar experiences. It is always comforting to know we are not alone in our exploration. Yvonne provides a safe place to explore, a community to share your experiences with, and assistance as you find your own voice.

Brenda Julian Williams, June 2020

Introduction

Sometime between 1995 and 1997, while living in Muncie, Indiana, I awoke one morning in the predawn hours to find a glowing blue triangle near the ceiling of my bedroom. I could see the image with my eyes opened or closed. The room was dark, and since I had been asleep I knew this was not a retinal persistence of vision. I felt the triangle as a supernatural presence, but there was something more to it. I would now call that something a "download." At the time, I was still trying to fit into religious circles; therefore, my understanding of what I was being shown was filtered through those lenses.

In my mind, I asked, Who or what are you? and immediately "heard" a response.

I am the angel that put out the fire the day you were burned.

I had always known a miracle had occurred that 21st day of October 1976. A grease fire had broken out in our kitchen, and was still burning when a neighbor drove me to the emergency room for treatment of the burns I had sustained. Later, I learned that when the firefighters, who we passed on the way to the hospital, arrived moments later they found the fire was completely out.

Tears of gratitude flooded my eyes as I continued to stare at the blue triangle.

Years later, and with more metaphysical understanding, I concluded that this presence was Archangel Michael. I now know that it was also a symbol of the Tri-Vector System™ that unites Spirit, body, and personality/ego. Working with the vector or triad wave allows us to return to Source or "Home." Source is the energy field from which all things come. During my coaching sessions that include light language, I have often transmitted that blue triangle symbol to clients who were prepared to receive its encoded message.

People are drawn to have sessions with me when they are ready for the wholistic tri-vector work designed to bring us through the 5th Element of unconditional love and to the 6th Element. If you were drawn to this book, you may already be a celestial shaman and doing some of the things outlined herein. If you are ready to have Spirit fully embodied in your physical form, you will find the concept of Celestial Shamanism™ as a source of practical knowledge, both for your personal ascension and to take to your clients, loved ones, and the masses.

Brenda Williams, a long-time friend of mine, came back into my life in 2019 when I moved to the southern part of Middle Tennessee. Brenda had traveled a lot over the years. One of her home bases was a little cabin about twenty minutes from my new home. She and I had been in touch off and on since we met in 2013. We knew there was work for us to do together—someday. Our newly arranged proximity allowed us to meet in person for some intense discovery sessions that brought downloads, ah-ha moments, and a renewed passion for the individual work each of us was doing. Both of us felt that we were moving into new territory. It became apparent that our "someday" had arrived and was bringing her scientific work as a technician together with my activation work as a practitioner of light codes. Brenda helped bring cohesiveness to my work by introducing me to the terminology of the triad or vector wave that moves in all directions and brings spirit, body, and personality into wholeness. Her excitement sparked my passion for finishing this book.

I began writing this book in 2014, shortly after publishing Light Language Emerging. The five years that followed brought countless miracles, transformative experiences, and downloads, both for myself and the people I work with, that I now realize were necessary for this book. Some parts came from presentation notes I created for the celestial shaman workshops I facilitated at Sweethome Retreat, the space my then-husband and I opened to those desiring to attend drum circles, potlucks, workshops, and art events, or to stay in our Air B&B. Indeed, people from all over the world were drawn to receive from the land and nature beings in the strong energy vortex there. Some people felt light-headed, expanded, or spacey when they walked into the chapel, a place designated to connect with multidimensional selves and higher dimensional light beings.

Then, in the latter part of 2019, I found myself single again and in a holding pattern while I rearranged my life. I was not sure if I would still offer spiritual retreats and drum circles at my new place like I had hosted at Sweethome. I was also undecided about whether to continue one-on-one coaching. Should I make more light language audios? Get back into creating music? Do more radio shows? Pursue in-person speaking engagements? Reopen my podcast? Take a job in retail or corporate? Where was Spirit leading me? I knew at some point I would complete this book, but I was not rushing it. This was a new phase in my life and the dust was still settling. Taking a break from everything I had been doing made the most sense. So, I rested physically and gave myself tender loving care that helped my personality adjust to all the changes. Engaging in creative projects like crocheting, sewing, drawing light codes, gardening, and decorating my new space gave me time to recalibrate.

I began combing through Interviews on a variety of topics that I had recorded with radio hosts and on tele-summits. As I listened and transcribed hours of information (including recorded conversations with Brenda), I received downloads and codes that are embedded in these pages. There was more to be said about walk-ins and light language from the perspective of the Concept. I have weaved that information into the content.

My coaching for empaths, walk-ins, light language speakers, and celestial shamans gave me a good understanding of spiritual awakenings, energy shifts, kundalini experiences, soul swaps, and other life-changing events that people were having. I was using light codes to help myself and clients bring the "higher self" into the physical form while integrating the personality, which many call the ego, shadow self, human self, lower aspect, inner child, and so on.

This book expanded as I progressed on my path. It covers a variety of topics from The Wholistic Concept, Tri-Vector System™, relationships, the 5th Element of unconditional love, the 6th Element of Home, light codes (the Keys to the Kingdom), Celestial Shamanism™, artistic expression, working with off-planet teams, and my personal journey through the ongoing ascension process. There is more than one way to do anything. I share my perspective to support you in making your own choices that have a lasting and positive impact.

We are moving from a head-knowledge and analytical experience of life on Earth to a telepathic heart-felt expression of our divinity—Spirit embodied in matter/flesh. Some of the things we now experience defy human logic, and that is necessary if we are to transcend our self-sabotaging and disempowering beliefs and move toward a greater and more intuitive knowing of our creative power. Much of what is presented here will be felt or realized telepathically. If you sense energy moving at any particular time while reading this material, please pause and receive the shift-gift.

I realized many years ago that I had been working with a team of off-planet technicians, programmers, geneticists, and etheric surgeons all of my adult life—possibly even as a child. In the span between my Earth incarnations, I sense that I have worked as an interplanetary ambassador with my teammates in other star regions. It never felt necessary for me to know their names or what genetic "race" they represented. They are from the multiverse and include Arcturian, Lyran, Syrian, Andromedan, Pleiadian, as well as other starseed groups. None of us is really a Pleiadian or Arcturian being, even if we resonate with them or have spent many lifetimes in that star system. That is not who we really are. We are aspects of Spirit having an experience in various frequency bands and density levels of matter.

I sense that my guides do not like to be called ETs or aliens. I started calling them my "Beloveds," which encompasses all my team members, no matter what field or dimension they are in. And it expresses my love and appreciation for them.

I tried several ideas regarding the main title of this book. What term encapsulates the interstellar work we are doing now? We travel celestially. We are taking shamanism to a unified level in concert with our human experience as we move out of the old paradigm. There are technical aspects to this type of shamanism, which can be supported scientifically. Hoping for this book to reach healers and lightworkers who are consciously in touch with multiverse off-planet teams, I decided to stay with "Celestial Shamanism™". This is the term I was given when I started sharing this process with others. Therefore, I trademarked the wholistic concept of Celestial Shamanism so people would be sure to find this version that relates to the fully integrated divine human.

So, onward we go.

CHAPTER 1 ~ What is a Celestial Shaman?

Celestial shamans are the modern-day prophets showing humanity what is possible when we remember our true nature and stop following dysfunctional trends and beliefs. Like ancient prophets, celestial shamans are on-the-ground liaisons for off-planet beings working through humans to perform what some consider to be miracles. Prophets and prophetesses were often viewed as strange or different because they did not adhere to the norms accepted by their society. They saw and heard things others did not. Their strong faith in their higher guidance propelled them forward as leaders in their world.

Dreams and foretelling visions directed humanity through the insight and messages given by these unusual mystics. Instead of dying, some ancient prophets were "taken up into heaven" (spaceships, most likely) and never seen again. Celestial shamans are the Spirit of Elijah that must come and already is. Many were incarnated angels that demonstrated an empowered way of operating as Spirit in human form.

Today, celestial priestesses and priests minister from the private temple of their heart—in the still point of infinite possibilities. These empowered lightworkers often gain wisdom and develop their healing modalities by intuitively following a trail of synchronic breadcrumbs. These trailblazers learn on the fly as they are instructed from lessons learned in their Earth experiences and from beings in higher realms. Many have not received formal training from traditional shamanic cultures—some are children. Their spiritual education often comes from harsh life experiences—many have survived abuse and trauma and wondered if they incarnated into the wrong family!

Celestial prophets are often rejected by friends and family who think of them as weird or mentally/emotionally unstable due to their sensitivities. As empaths, they may have taken on the burdens of others before they realized it was about to kill them. Once they learned new ways to transmute energy, they became or are becoming the healers that the rest of the world looks to when conventional medicine and talk therapies do not help.

Children and adults with shamanic abilities know things they have not learned. They see, feel, hear, smell, and taste with heightened senses. In other words, they have psychic abilities/spiritual gifts. Being energy-sensitive, they are aware of non-physical realms. They know when someone is lying because they read energy instead of lips. They communicate telepathically through the language of vibration. They are in touch with the Universal Mind and have a close connection with nature, animals, and beings in higher realms of consciousness. They know their own heart and consistently purify and re-direct wayward thoughts.

Sound familiar? That is because I am talking about YOU! The celestial shamans on Earth now are you and me! We have lived in other star systems within the multiverse in various humanoid or non-human forms. We are starseeds incarnated into human form to help raise the human consciousness on Planet Earth. Solo practitioners, healers of humanity, lightworkers—regardless of the label we give ourselves—we are the ones we have been waiting for. We are here to hold a resonant field and offer a hand up to those who are just beginning to awaken.

Most people perceive things happening linearly. Scientists, however, are now moving their understanding from a chronological view of time toward a simultaneous one on various dimensional bandwidths. Etheric counterparts or holographic aspects of consciousness are interacting across time-space. Thus, you may begin to recognize your multidimensional selves on a quantum level where things behave differently than they do in 3-D reality. Due to the cyclical nature of the universe, you may embody future or parallel selves in this lifetime, which creates a huge shift in your personality, likes, and dislikes. Others may think something is terribly wrong with you. Naturally, you may feel confused when you encounter yourself in simultaneous lifetimes or move across timelines that maintain various bandwidths. This practice will become more comfortable and normal as you acclimate to being in the still-point field.

Celestial shamans recognize and integrate multidimensional forms and expressions of spirit and personality. Many of us allow consciousnesses from our soul group or spirit team to walk in or through our physical body. We see the body as a vessel that operates behind a veil that is becoming thinner as the consciousness of humanity raises. We deal with archetypes and expressions of the ego/personality as a normal part of the Earth experience. We feel, smell, and even taste energy. We hear voices, and sometimes they have conversations with one another in languages we do not understand. How we respond to the senses of our inner terrain is what determines our external experience. One who is able to befriend the voices and lovingly realign the shadow side of the personality can live an empowered life without fear. He or she can maintain inner peace even in the midst of external chaos.

Honoring the code of ethics found in the Original Directives, Celestial Shamanism™ is the work done by starseeds who have incarnated for the purpose of assisting with creating the New Earth. Keenly guided by our intuition or spirit, we interact with our off-planet loved ones and teammates with whom we exchange codes, symbols, frequencies, sounds, colors, mathematical formulas, geometric structures, and transmissions that affect change on a quantum level.

Jesus Christ is quoted as saying, "In my father's house are many mansions. If it were not so, I would have told you." These mansions could be levels of density or frequency bands in which we can make an appearance or live in various forms. Imagine the Earth surrounded by twelve concentric circles or various bandwidths of density, color, and frequency. In these levels are units of Source, which have the form of angels, archangels, fairies, elementals, nature spirits, portal guardians, wisdom keepers, guardians, and sub-units of souls created by monads (oversouls). Crew members on lightships in these bandwidths include ethereal technicians, surgeons, DNA programmers, geneticists, celestial mappers, grid keepers, and so on. It is possible to move upward into less-compressed dimensions surrounding this planet. This span of movement depends upon unification of spirit, body, and personality, which holds a vibrational signature. A person's afterlife existence continues in bandwidths that resonate with the level best suited for the soul's continuing exploration.

Heavier or denser circles are closest to the Earth and beam the program or patterns of karma toward the residents on the planet. In her book, The Pleiadian Workbook: Awakening Your Divine Ka, Amorah Quan Yin mentions seven primary karmic patterns that need to be transcended: arrogance, addiction, prejudice, hatred, violence, victimhood, and shame. All these go against the "do no harm" in the Original Directives established by the multiverse. These ego allurements are the seven seals that must be opened or loosened (alchemized) in order to attain full enlightenment. The ego/shadow side is currently being exaggerated in order to bring awareness to the areas that contain patterns which are being transformed across the globe.

There are no lightships outside the bandwidth circles nearest to Earth because there is no need for a physical container for consciousness to move throughout the multiverses. Higher intelligence, or sentience, moves at the speed of light and sound without the limitations of a body or form. The higher a being resides in the dimensions, the less density they hold. The beings of lighter density have a higher level of perspective, expertise, knowledge, and sphere of influence.

Everything on the planet is indirectly guided from off planet. Outside the Earth circle, everything is consciousness and beings there are beyond a plasma state or etheric form. They exist as rainbow spectrum colors, harmonic frequencies, rays, and pure consciousness. They are identified by sound and geometric signatures that humans are not able to hear or vocalize. The off-planet teams of unified consciousness that work with starseed shamans on the ground exist outside and beyond the vibratory rings of Earth.

Traditional shamans are sometimes called medicine men or women. I will refer to them as Earth shamans in my attempt to clarify and compare their roles to those of a modern-day celestial shaman. Earth shamans use medicinal plants, incantations, charms, stones, bones, and ceremony to connect with spirit world (including guides and ancestors) and/or work with the Earth and nature. This is done in order to treat disease, clear family issues, or receive guidance on life situations using methods and traditions that have been passed down through elders. While there is a faster and better way to treat misaligned energy patterns, the traditional methods were the only way our ancestors knew to try to restore the fallen human condition.

Earth shamans are able to move throughout dimensions (levels of consciousness) surrounding and inside the Earth. Hallucinogenic drugs may be used to induce altered states of consciousness in order to journey to other levels of reality. Many are able to travel while maintaining conscious presence in the physical body. Some are shape- shifters, which means they can assume the form of another animal, person, or object.

Ancient Earth shamans originally worked with off-planet beings that they called "star nations." They understood and practiced unity with all things cosmic and on Mother Earth. Carl Johan Calleman wrote about "Unity Shamanism," which honors, harmonizes, and unifies forces that appear to be in opposition to one another. Celestial shamans are moving back to Unity Shamanism, which is individual physical, emotional, and mental connection with Source. When religion took control of native practices, shamanism moved from unity, or oneness, to an imbalanced masculine interpretation. In recent attempts to counterbalance an overbearing male energy, the power switch has flipped to the feminine. What we need is harmonization, in which we love and honor both aspects of our divinity, without placing more value on one than the other.

Celestial shamans are connected with specific (or more than one) star groups, planetary systems, or celestial races. Some collaborate with high-vibrational beings in multiverse sectors where they open and close portals on Earth and in time-space dimensions. They move through star gates that are accessed with vector codes or geometric time-space codes for those dimensions. A vector code is a time and space representative or consciousness placeholder where cellular "memory" or coordinates are held. This is why so many celestial shamans use light language symbols or sound frequencies in their work.

As a celestial shaman, you may perform all the duties of an Earth shaman. We can channel energy from various bandwidths or conscious levels, which is then shared at a quantum level with Earth and her inhabitants. During the early years of our spiritual development, many of us encountered deceased human spirits in the dimensions closest to the planet. Some become mediums and use this as a gift to humanity. Some celestial shamans carry a portal in their personal field that allows them to cross souls over to the next bandwidth/dimension of the Earth plane after the death of the body. Others read the Akashic records and do past-life regressions, which accesses the vibrational timeline incarnations that may be bleeding through like watercolors to this lifetime. Some have the gift of healing in their hands, and others have the gift of reading or seeing energy. You may conduct rituals, hold lunar cycle ceremonies, perform mediumship, go on shamanic journeys, and channel information from inside the Earth and surrounding density levels or circles. All of our tools and gifts are useful and needed. When you use traditional tools, you may feel led to employ them in intuitive new ways. Use physical tools when they are available, but know that you are still able to do your work without them.

1 Thessalonians 4:16-18 (KJV) is a Bible scripture that says, "For the Lord Himself shall descend from heaven with a shout, with the voice of the archangel, and with the Trump of God: and the dead in Christ shall rise first: Then we which are alive and remain shall be caught up together with them in the clouds, to meet the Lord in the air: and so shall we ever be with the Lord. Wherefore comfort one another with these words."

I want to dissect this passage because there is so much relevance to our current world conditions. I believe this in-depth plunge will help us see our role as first-wave and second-wave ascenders. According to Matt Kahn, the first-wavers are not warriors—they hold the frequency of love, light, and peace to counterbalance the un-doing of anti-Christ systems. The second-wavers are grassroots leaders, peaceful protestors, and activists that are doing the work of social reform. Both are equally important.

- The "shout of the Lord" descended upon humanity in a noticeable way at the start of 2020—the year of clear vision. The forcefield around Earth that has held the frequencies of arrogance, addiction, prejudice, hatred, violence, victimhood, and shame is being dismantled as injustices are brought to the Light. Systems that have kept humans enslaved are being replaced by the 5th Element of unconditional love.

- The Christ Consciousness is rising in our voices—the codes of light are being spoken by many. The archangelic voice of higher consciousness is creating global changes in economics, healthcare, race relations, workplace practices, and every social expression and interaction among humans.
- I am stepping out on a limb here to say that the "Trump of God" is Donald Trump. Since before his election as President of the United States of America, I saw him as anti-Christ because everything he stands for is against the loving teachings of Jesus. I now see "Trump" being played as if in a partnership with the Divine—a role similar to Judas Iscariot in Jesus' day. Trump was never meant to be a leader who would create world peace, but rather a destroyer of our complacency with how things were. His finger-pointing to the seven primary karmic patterns of Earth has certainly gotten our attention and incited us to action. Collectively, he is inciting people to decide whether they want world peace or world destruction. This one trumpet/man has exposed more darkness on our planet and in individual hearts and minds than anyone in the past. The 5th Element of Love will one day rule human hearts as we interact with one another on Earth or beyond.
- The dead in Christ are those who are stuck in the Earth plane without a body to inhabit. We are encouraged to forgive their karma and cross these Earthbound souls into the light or higher dimensions, where they can continue to evolve without interfering with the ascension of humanity.
- We who are alive and remain will be drawn upward into light ships, which are often cloaked in cloud

formations to be in a place prepared for us by Christ. Jesus was taken up in a cloud that received Him out of sight. Two men in white apparel stood by witnesses and said, "This same Jesus, which is taken up from you into heaven, shall so come in like manner as ye have seen Him go into heaven." (Acts 1: 9-11) In order to ascend like this, we need a light body. We are not ascending our soul. Our soul is a perfect image of God. We are ascending our body and personality.

"For those of you who have mastered the behavioral and attitudinal levels of these patterns, or are sincerely working on them, your next step is conscious of alignment with your higher self, higher collective consciousness, and divine oneness."

~ Amorah Quan Yin

As starseed shamans, we assist in evolving the human body and its personality. Our intent is to usher in the divine human form as an activated light body having less density and attachment to materialism. Free will is still very much a part of the new human experience. But, with less detrimental coding in the personality it becomes easier to make compassionate choices that benefit the Earth and all her inhabitants. Overriding obsolete coding is a process that integrates spirit, body, and personality through loving treatment of whatever arises. Our work allows everyone to ascend authentically as each person discovers the sacred part of their own divine nature.

A celestial shaman can produce a wave with vector properties that can detect and realign patterns contained in old stories about self-worth or inferiority complex patterns.

We can erase, resolve, or override energetic virus codes (often referred to as karma or curses) from previous experiences. These codes may be in the body, the DNA, electromagnetic field, or elsewhere. In the physical body, the codes are reorganized in the neural pathways of the brain and in the emotional body as it relates to the personality. This re-scripting may install new codes to support the upgraded human form. The templates of the human body and the grids (or information highway) of the Earth are constantly being upgraded.

Celestial shamans are blazing new paths on Earth as we work with off-planet beings to restore the human template of DNA to its original divine state before tampering occurred and caused anomalies. This restoration naturally opens our awareness to other realms and offers us the ability to manage energy more consciously. Manifesting becomes easier and faster. However, our main purpose here is to love unconditionally and consistently hold the vibration of the 5th Element of Love. Thus, it is important to stay connected to Spirit and recognize when the human self (personality) is in the driver's seat. Like Christ and other prophets, we are here to show humanity what is possible when we remember our true nature and surrender to a higher love. Surrendering the personality to Source does not mean loss. We do not lose anything but our internal struggle. We gain insight and joy as we learn to cooperate and flow with higher love.

CHAPTER 2 ~ Old Traditions, New Ways

In other civilizations, humans have used technology much more advanced than what we currently have at our disposal. The US government has been working with galactic technology since before World War II. This is obvious in the rapid manner in which technology and military tactics have been advancing over the last decades. But our technology is still device-based, rather than inwardly connected and applied. We have advanced biotechnology within our spirit and body. We are bio-computers, but we are still trying to operate in older systems. Using old formats is like trying to use a dial-up service on an outdated computer. You may be able to send an email (or not) but it will be much slower, and you will not be able to send a file of any size. Many of our beliefs and practices on this planet do not support the correct three-part system of spirit, body, and personality. The vibrational fields or communication grids on earth have been hijacked. This is why so many people feel blocked or that they cannot access their higher guidance.

We have done the best we could to get our individual pieces of the information puzzle on the table. Many healers are still using traditional tools that focus on external rules that must be followed exactly. For example, I evidently offended some indigenous people on YouTube when I posted a video on how to use sage for smudging. That was not my intention.

I am not much for rules and regulations—that is one of the reasons I left organized religion. I follow my inner guidance and work on the inner planes to create an outer effect. Smudging has worked fine for me. So has my medicine wheel, through which I did celestial portal work with my team. I did not call the four directions very often in that circle. I spoke light language before entering and could immediately feel the presence of higher vibrations. When it was time to work in the wheel, I would feel called to it. It was not an event on my calendar, it did not line up with any moon phase. I just intuitively knew when it was time. I would often get pictures in my mind as to what materials to bring into the circle, which way to walk within the circle, which direction to face, and what to do as a follow-up. I no longer have a medicine wheel at my house. I now carry the vortex and energy of that space in my body/field and can call upon it anytime. The tools celestial shamans use are inside us—we simply need to attune our body and field to carry their etheric blueprint.

While living at Sweethome, I allowed several different practitioners to present their work in classes, workshops, and events. One Cree native desired to have a sweat lodge as part of our fall gathering. I had no idea there were so many dos and don'ts in setting up the space! I was reprimanded for not wearing the right clothing and for crossing the imaginary line that no one mentioned was there. I was told that no photos could be taken at any point during the setup or the ceremony.

Once inside the tent we had constructed, I had a lot of thoughts to examine. Why was I feeling like I wanted to run out of the tent? It was not the heat—I had stayed the full round in sweat lodges before. I felt trapped, just as I had in church where I had to conform to the rules set by the "leadership." So, this was a trigger for me.

After the first round was complete, I went to the woods to check my personal 18-inch energy field and inquire of my guides if I should go back in for another round. I felt light-hearted in the woods but when I thought about going back into that tent I felt uncomfortable energy in my body. I did not participate in the second round and continued to seek guidance on what I was experiencing.

I am not sure how many rounds were conducted. I came back hours later and attended the last round because I felt like I needed to support the facilitator and be a good example to the others who were enjoying the ceremony and were benefitting from sweating. My spirit, body, and personality were shouting in unison that this ceremony was not for me. I had to interrupt and be let out of the tent.

The next day, the leaders took the tobacco prayer bags used in the ceremony and tied them to the trees in the woods in my backyard. After they left, I videoed the prayer ties in a walkabout in the forest. I was singing and speaking light language and giving gratitude for the fall retreat and everyone who had attended. I sent the video in a private email only to those who had participated in the sweat lodge, thanking them for coming. I was again reprimanded when the leader saw the video. My heart sank. I had not recognized the value of honoring the traditions of the Cree people. What felt like restrictive rules to me may be survival strategies for Native peoples whose cultures were nearly destroyed by White settlers. There is a lot of valid upset in Indigenous communities around that. I understand why they desire to preserve their sacred traditions from dilution or misuse by outsiders like me.

Everyone has their own methods and opinions—mine are no better or less correct than anyone else's. In all circumstances, find what works for you. It is fine for others to have an experience different from yours. Allow your beliefs and practices to change as you learn, grow, and evolve.

Ayahuasca, DMT, and Plant Medicine

The love revolution of the 1960s awakened the world to recognize the value of emotional and spiritual connections. Similar to the way drugs and sex did back then, ayahuasca, magic mushrooms, DMT (N,N-Dimethyltryptamine), and certain plant medicines are used by those on a spiritual path today. DMT is a substance contained in some plant species, which have been used in religious ceremonies in South American countries for centuries. Psychedelics take people out of body and give them glimpses into other dimensions. That can be useful at times, but most people are not in their bodies to begin with and have no idea that they are paying money and traveling long distances to experience what they already have inside.

We came here to evolve while on this planet and to set in place a reality that could be replicated and utilized in every walk of life. Not everyone can afford to use plant medicine as a tool for enlightenment. It is good to know that we can be creative and in alignment with Spirit without the use of substances. Altered states of consciousness can be achieved through embodying Spirit. We can fully experience life by tuning into all our senses.

Embodiment means "in the body"—spirit inside the body. We cannot reach 6th Element embodiment without being in the body. We use our internal wisdom and innate sensory abilities to unify spirit, body, and personality. All that being said, I have known people who opened their personal light language during ceremonies that involved respectful use of plant medicine. People have also experienced beneficial releases of emotional energy. One woman told me she had the most phenomenal experience on mushrooms as she merged with universal intelligence. She sat by the water's edge and saw geometric light codes dancing in the water. So, follow your heart on this and all things, but also know that you can embody the spiritual essence or code of any sacred tool or plant.

A few years ago, I decided to have an energy session with Veronica O'Grady, my dear shaman friend. As I was on her treatment table, she sat at the head of the table transmitting energy into my crown. I begin to have a vision of a Peruvian shaman coming to me. He offered me a bowl of what I instinctively knew was ayahuasca. I did not want to take it from him. I had heard how it makes people throw up and I absolutely abhor returning partially-digested groceries!

Nevertheless, I saw myself reluctantly accept the bowl of plant medicine from the shaman. I drank all of it, then heard the shaman say something to the effect that "You now carry the energy of the medicine." I thought nothing more of it as a lay there on the table receiving wonderful vibrations and waves of relaxation as Veronica worked on my field and body.

Suddenly, I started feeling sick to my stomach. I did not know if I was going to throw up or have diarrhea or both. I interrupted Veronica, saying, "I have to go to the bathroom now!" I jumped off the table and before I could get around the corner I had already shit my pants!! And, as I had not planned to ingest a dose of etheric ayahuasca, I did not bring a change of clothes. I had to ask Veronica to get me something to clean myself and her bathroom. I left for home wearing a towel, my dirty clothes stuffed into a grocery bag.

Afterward, I wondered/doubted if this unexpected purging had anything to do with the bowl of plant brew I had taken only in my spirit vision. I had never had this kind of reaction from energy work before. How could the essence of the plant have that kind of effect upon my physical body? Was my imagination that powerful, or did I actually engage with this shaman in another dimension?

A few weeks later, my clients started mentioning that they were experiencing a trancelike state while I worked on them distantly through Skype or the phone. Clients reported having breakthroughs and emotional healing. Many told me it felt like I came into their field or moved energetically through their physical body as I drummed, sang, and spoke light language to them. Intuitively, I knew that this was the result of that experience I had that day at Veronica's. I was learning first-hand what a shaman named Tucah had told me when she broke an expensive crystal bowl.

"I do not need the bowl as a tool anymore," she said without a trace of emotion, "I have embodied its essence."

Sometimes we need to let go of something we held onto before we can gain better understanding. My beliefs continue to shift as I learn new things. I find it helpful to sit with incoming information to see what is similar to and different from what I already believe. Most of it is a matter of terminology—a different way of saying something I already know. For example, the field that Brenda and I refer to as "our personal 18 inches" is referred to as "the vortex" by Abraham Hicks. I try to look for similarities when something new comes across my awareness. If there is some new nugget of truth that resonates with my spirit, I will add it to my repertoire. New perspective brings new practice.

In the past, I hesitated to promote the books I wrote years ago because the information seemed old or outdated to me. For example, since writing Whose Stuff Is This?, I have learned more effective ways to deal with emotions and embrace my sensitive nature; I also know a lot more about the walk-in process. Then I realized that my older books and information may help someone move away from limiting beliefs and listen to their own guidance. When I first left organized religion there was an emptiness in my life that urged me to find answers within myself. When people are ready for the next step, they will find the resources that can best support the next part of their journey.

There are times when I am given the password to a client's energy field. This allows my energy to go in like a cleaning device and shift things in their body, personality, past experiences, ancestral line, or Akashic records. This is the movement of the blue triangle that carries vector energy. People have said it felt like I was inside their body. This is interesting, for while I feel altered and relaxed during these sessions I certainly do not feel like I am in their body. To me, it feels like we are connecting our auras at a higher level and creating a resonate field or vibrational opportunity in which to allow the person to unite their body with their spirit.

There is a difference between your aura and your personal 18-inch field. Your aura (electromagnetic field) can extend, expand, morph, and connect with others in a resonant field. This blending of energy fields allows creative minds to collaborate and to communicate telepathically. I might also mention that mixed auras can feel very chaotic. This discord is what you feel in a public setting where people are not on the same wavelength and you are allowing your aura to interact with theirs. Your personal 18 inches is your sovereign territory and should be diligently guarded to avoid contamination. It is seen as a cylinder of light surrounding the body. It is open to Source/Cosmos at the top, and open at the bottom to allow connection with Mother Earth.

It was not uncommon for Earth shamans to take illness and other dense energy forms out of a person's body and transmute it through their own physical vessel or personal field. I have held space while a shaman puked in my backyard after doing some intense energy work. I have witnessed the power of this technique, but I do not sense that it is the best way to transmute energy. I envision any energy that is coming out of a client's field as being sucked into a funnel-like vortex filled with violet flames. I call the vortex into place above my head as I work with clients. The wider opening of the funnel is closer to my head with the tapered end facing upward. As energy is drawn through the wide end of vortex it is transmuted before exiting out the top. The fountain of gold sparkling energy cascades out the top of the funnel and into my personal field where I reclaim the converted energy to propel the energy session. Like a battery that stores solar power, this recycled/transmuted energy can be held with intention to be used for personal support. This keeps me from being drained by the work that I do.

Old shamanism keeps people relying upon shamans and healers to fix messes. Those who see themselves as less powerful still rely upon someone else to do their clearing for them. You have everything needed to do your unification work. If someone asks for your help, teach them how to transform their personality to be in harmony and absolute resonance with spirit. Individual transformation is an inside job that we can maintain in our own physiology. While we can certainly hold a vibrational field for someone while they access their own healing power and shift their perspective, transformation comes from their personal connection with spirit.

Holding space for someone means that we are willing to walk alongside them in whatever journey they are on without judging them, making them feel inadequate, trying to fix them, or hoping to impact outcomes. We open our hearts, offer unconditional support, and let go of judgment and control. This brings freedom to us as our focus and time is spent on getting to know ourselves and feel our own energy within our personal field, which is ready to support our personal transformation from the inside out. The coding for transmuting dense vibrations is in the template or blueprint for the fully integrated human. We have received enough upgrades to handle our own return to Source. The masses that have never been ready before are beginning to be ready now. There are no distortions in the overall Earth ascension project, which ended in 2012 according to the Mayan calendar. While the project is complete in its perfection, we are yet to experience it to its fullest. This is why we feel like there is more clearing and healing to be done.

You likely found yourself on the celestial shaman path quite naturally and may not know when or how you started moving energy. You may have progressed into the awareness through experiences and dark nights of the soul that felt like initiations. Unlike Reiki or other modalities that are taught and offer a certification, the role of a celestial shaman is a self-evolved model that incorporates the life experiences, skillsets, talents, and spiritual gifts of multiple lifetimes. This book is encoded with frequencies to enhance the gifts you already operate in, and open more that are ready to be called into service. Pause and draw in that activation.

Because of the intuitive and prophetic nature and the personal initiation that awakens the potency of a celestial shaman, there is no specific training course that can give you the ability to carry the "anointing" bestowed upon you. Like most spiritual gifts, the amount of power a celestial shaman can hold and transmit is a result of how well one maintains their own energy. It may come from personality refinement that has been accomplished over many lifetimes.

A celestial shaman's dormant mantle can be reactivated. If you have shut down gifts or stopped using them, they can be resurrected. If you desire more embodiment of Spirit, if you are purifying your personality, and if you are practicing unconditional love to the best of your ability, you are already being reactivated. Being in the presence and energy of an individual or group that is already moving in the gift of 5th Element Love helps expand and deepen your anointing. Many are called, but few choose to answer. And even fewer are ready to step into the celestial shamanic role due to the level of surrender it requires. The programming of the personality will try to stop you from making the commitment to trust Source and your intuitive guidance.

Answering the call naturally requires the body to shift in order to house and hold frequency upgrades. Big life changes and walk-ins could be part of that process. Celestial shamans are consistently updating their operating system and bringing in more evolved versions of their divine expression of consciousness. Etheric members of the celestial team may rotate in or out of the physical body (a portal in itself) to offer support or service. We will talk about that in the chapter on walk-ins.

CHAPTER 3 ~ The Concept and Original Directives

"In the beginning" was the sound that gives form to vibration and the silence that guides us home. It is Alpha and Omega, the beginning that goes out and the ending that comes home to start again as it continues to cycle and expand. It is Source (some call it God), the zero-point field of nothing where everything is possible.

Undifferentiated Source is too vast to fit into one body form or planet. Therefore, matter (various frequencies of solid form) was created from the nothingness to allow Source to have experiences in all formats—everythingness. From rocks and insects to flowers and trees, from animals and humans to angels and archangels, matter began to form various expressions throughout the multiverses, which Source also created. So began the formation of sentient beings.

As Source began to animate (breathe life into) its creation, twelve geometric oversouls containing holographic identities of Source were created. The twelve oversouls became creators, sending up to twelve virtual fractals known as higher-self souls to explore the multiverse. These twelve higher selves also created replica souls that manifested into denser (more solid) forms having different levels of sentience or awareness of itself as Source. Each soul would need to start at the bottom level of density and move upward through circles or rings of consciousness in order to return Home to Source. In this book, I will refer to this homecoming as the 6th Element. As humans in our current expression or lifetime, we are part of a vast number of parallel souls or soul aspects playing out scenarios throughout the multiverse. We are all on our way back to Source, even as Source continues to expand. It is like the inhale and the exhale of our bodies—going out and coming back.

As the multiverse came into being, the oversouls considered how humans could have experiences in various density levels that allow all of them to grow and create a unique reality. The big picture for the human-on-Earth experience contained Original Directives. It was decided that humans would be allowed to judge their experiences as good or a bad, defined a value system they would create. Humans would have freedom to explore and the multiverse would not hold that against them—even if someone wanted to have a bad experience. They would also have free will to live their lives in joy and peace and associate with whomever they wish. They could follow their inner spirit guidance or give their decision-making power to another person—meaning they could allow someone to tell them how to conduct their lives. The main directive was "Do no harm," or "Do unto others as you would have them do unto you." In other words, trust Source, love yourself, and love others. As celestial shamans, we have pledged to live by the Original Directives and have been doing so all along. To us, it makes no sense why anyone would not live by them. Yet, being constantly submerged in the distorted vibrational frequencies of the human collective mindset, our personality has its own agenda and is often out of resonance with our soul and spirit.

Most people have heard about these directives in religious, social, and moral training, but not all have followed them. We were given an empirical state of consciousness in the beginning. Remembering, knowing, and being curious about life creates the design of our human experience. It is our personality in form. The oversouls explored how misconceptions around falling from that state of innocence/remembrance could be dealt with. What would happen if human reality should differ from the Original Directives, which are non-judgmental and inclusive?

Our human brain was originally designed as a statistical database, much like a computer, to categorize the information received from our sensory receptors. It was originally designed to work in concert with our free will. As we have experienced, the concept of free will has been compromised and entrained to the will of another.

As we grow from childhood to adult, our personality begins to conform to the rules and expectations of what we are shown, taught, told, and expected to believe. As we assimilate, decode, process, and act upon information or data received through our many sensory receptors, we formulate the information as our experience. As we move further into this process, we will recognize the significance of our complex design and its ability to reset and self-adjust to whatever our divine matrix codes has brought us here to experience.

It is up to each of us to determine if our life experiences are similar to or different from the information we have accumulated in our database from what we have been told and what we have learned. Does what you now believe resonate with your inner knowing or the Original Directives that gave you free will? In the midst of change in our world that seems chaotic, we are approaching a time in our evolutionary process that opens the opportunity and potential to return to our original operating system and move within the wisdom of the 6th Element.

Vector vs. Scalar

People may be familiar with Nikola Tesla's work with scalar, which has thrust in one direction. Scalar size is specified by just one magnitude or single number. For example: length, time, temperature, speed, velocity, mass, or density. Scalar frequency can kill a cancer cell; but if that is the only frequency you are using it may not sustain itself. The body may produce more cancer cells. Because it can only move one way, scalar cannot work with the multiple levels of our physiology. Nor can it bring our spiritual, physical, and science into one concept.

Vector is movement that has both size (magnitude) and direction, for example, force and velocity. The vector begins a cycle and comes back in three different (3D) ways. Light language, and the three-sided blue triangle energy code that I downloaded in Muncie, carry vector movement. It is accessing everything as it bypasses the primitive brain that is constantly wanting to tell it what to do. As vector energy moves through a person's body and electromagnetic field it finds anomalies. This allows the whole system to adjust and move through larger bandwidths. As a result, we adjust our internal routing (bioacoustics) and how we move within our

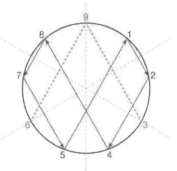

external (eco-acoustic) environment.

Nikola Tesla worked with vortex-based math in which numerals 1, 2, 4, 5, 7, and 8 follow a sequence that cannot be broken. They relate to physical life. The vortex triangle of 3, 6, and 9, also known as the Key to the Universe, relates to Spirit. Like so many scientists, Tesla applied his triangle theory to devices, not the physical body. Each scientist gets a little bit of information and puts it into what they are familiar with. In doing so, our external technology advances, but there is no wholistic concept of the human form and its ability to integrate spirit and personality.

"As we begin to look at our Earth life experience in a wholistic way, there are several definitions that will form the bridges to our understanding. The first is tri-vector, which will become the platform upon which we build. The use of the word tri-vector moves between physics, spirituality, and physiology for it speaks to all three systems carefully integrated and clear about their individual tasks while always moving in resonance with the wholistic form. In physics, vector simply means moving multi-directional—it has both magnitude and direction and has the ability to increase/decrease the force or magnitude. As we proceed you will see how that is essential to the full assimilation, decoding, and processing of information within our original design in a resonant way that allows all systems to move without interference."

~ A Wholistic Concept, developed by Brenda Julian Williams

RBQT-18" is part of the Tri-Vector System™, which was developed by Brenda Julian Williams. It works with the original routing system in our human form and with the wisdom of our beginning. Notice the harmonics of three representing the vortex triangle: Reset Breath©, Quiet Touch™, and the 18-inch personal field. These three harmonics use a platform that is resonant with the way our human form was created. When we touch a part of our body, we draw our attention to it. Quiet Touch asks you to touch your heart/chest with your left palm and your abdomen with your right hand. Reset Breath©, which is not breathwork, asks you to stop whatever you are doing and pause. Our normal breathing pattern is an inhale followed by an exhale. The Reset Breath© begins with an exhale. Breaking the automatic breath cycle alerts the brain that a change is being made and that it needs to integrate new information.

1. Begin by exhaling through your mouth, keeping your eyes open.
2. Next, inhale through your nose, bringing the breath deep into your diaphragm while keeping your shoulders relaxed. Follow the breath as it moves through your body, filling the lungs and moving further.
3. At your own pace, exhale fully and completely through your mouth. Feel the still-point. This is where the synchronized sympathetic-parasympathetic balance of the body engages to join the personality and spirit. The entire system comes together to assimilate, decode, and process new information not based upon prior experiences.

Resume normal breathing and continue to engage with your physical senses.

The Reset Breath© is the foundational piece that sets the physical routing system to recognize the importance of the sympathetic and parasympathetic balance. Not only does this create optimum well-being and connection with our higher wisdom, it also creates a healing chemistry in the body that helps us feel safe. The body and personality cannot feel safe by affirming, "I feel safe." It only feels safe when it experiences the feeling of safety.

To further this experience, add quiet touch and focus on your 18-inch personal field of energy for a few moments.

> "When a healer, with the intent to heal, brings his hands close to, but not touching the healer, the brain waves of the healer comes into resonance within seconds, showing a peak power spectrum of 8Hz."
>
> ~ Dr. Andrija "Henry" Puharich

Some healers transmit a strong magnitude of vector. They can also receive, transduce, and hold higher vibrations more easily than others. I have found that some clients are more easily affected by a transmission than others. Their body may tingle or shake, emotions may burst forth, or they may have a familiar feeling of being "home." In other words, they reach the still-point and allow change to happen. Sometimes, the client is wiped out for the rest of the day (or for several days) as the body adjusts and integrates to the vector energy.

In numerous energy sessions, I have asked my Beloveds to "allow this person's body to be able to house and hold higher frequencies on an ongoing basis." When we begin to work with vector energy in every circumstance, things shift fast and continue to hold the new frequency pattern. I want my clients to be able to continue to do the work for themselves rather than create dependency upon me.

Other clients seem to feel little or nothing. That is not to say that the wave is not being broadcasted. There could be subconscious resistance that blocks or hinders movement within the person's body or field. The ability to receive and maintain higher frequencies depends upon the stability in one's foundation or personal energy field. If the foundation is not in balance, you or your client may not be able to maintain upgrades because the body will be sending mixed signals. The minute you hit a bump in the collective field, the body reverts to its former condition. This is not because there is error in your work, but because you are still working at a level of belief that something is wrong and needs to be fixed.

If a healer is working from the concept of wholeness, their client can quickly move to a new level and stay there. Practitioners who work from higher levels typically do not struggle or worry about results. The Tri-Vector System™ does all the heavy lifting. We may feel the need to rest and integrate afterward, which is a good practice for anyone. Since I stopped trying to do all the work for the client, I rarely feel tired after transmitting energy via light language.

I have heard nurses, masseurs/masseuses, and physical therapists tell me they become exhausted after working on other people's bodies. When a client or patient's auric field is open and relaxed, energy can be released into the shared collective field outside the body. If a practitioner is not maintaining his or her own personal 18 inches or cylinder of energy, he or she may take in energy from a client who is releasing toxic energy from the cells of their body. If you experience this, I encourage you to envision the funnel-like vortex filled with violet flames above you (described previously) when you do your work. Also, use the Reset Breath© throughout the session if you feel a client's energy is pushing on your field. This is one of those times when you may need to take command of the field you are working in and transmit energy to them as vibrations from higher realms flow through you. In other words, push their energy out of your field and into the transmutation funnel as you maintain your personal 18 inches.

When we live as the completed version of ourselves, we allow the heavens to shower blessings upon us as we stand at the top of the apex. There is no need for clearing or protection when your body and personality are surrendered to Spirit and connected to the zero-point field. All remains in perfect and divine order. Life flows easily.

Source, Spirit, Personality, and Body

If you refer to mind, body, spirit as the three parts of wholeness, you do not have all the puzzle pieces. You will continue to search and have an endless feeling that you are missing something. The three systems of wholeness are spirit/soul, body, and personality. Spirit, body, and personality function together as mind. The wholistic process of returning to Source requires us to integrate all three.

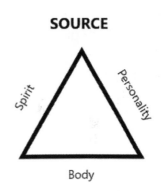

- Spirit or soul is our individual spark from Source
- Body is the physical form
- Personality is created through experience

Source

Above the triangle in this drawing is the empirical soul—the big brain directing the human experience. I will call it "Source" or "All That Is" since most people can relate to those terms. This is the zero-point field from which Spirit and all things emanate. Source is too powerful and vast to fit into one body. In order to experience form or matter, Source differentiates into multiple units known as "spirit," or soul.

Spirit

On the left side of the triangle in the drawing, Spirit enters the world in the form of a human. Excited about the potential that lies ahead, Spirit is filled with curiosity and willingness to experience and experiment. Spirit, like a child, is a blank slate in the beginning. Children are fearless. They explore and allow their curiosity to lead them.

Spirit comes into a body (as a baby or a walk-in) and immediately begins to be programmed by the emotional field (thoughts, feelings, and energy patterns) of its family and parents—especially the mother who is carrying the child inside her body. After the baby is born or the walk-in soul comes in, it continues to interact with family, peers, world systems, religious beliefs, etc. The personality picks up programming glitches that distort the truth of its identity as a unit of Source having a human Earth experience. Poor self-esteem and a lack of self-worth are the results of accepting limiting beliefs presented to us.

To a child, there are no anomalies or faults until programming begins. Personality believes what it is told. "You can do this. You cannot do that." Therefore, we manage our personality through emotions based on what somebody told us. Once information comes to the brain, it does not let go. If we believe our inner child has been wounded, we will continue to focus on healing it without realizing that from a higher perspective the work is already done. I realize that we live in dual or multiple timeline realities. We can see both timelines—the one in which we are healed and the one in which we are still struggling to be free. How about we remind ourselves that we are perfect just the way we are?

When we work with the triangle vector, we experience emotion and allow ourselves to interact with it even if it is not a favorable feeling. During an emotional upset is a good time to pause and explore any feelings of sadness or anger. Rub your palms together and allow the energy to be felt in the hands. Move your hands apart and back to center slowly several times. Notice how energy begins to rise between your hands as if a ball of energy is pulsing. This is your personal field or vortex around your body. Discern how it is similar and different when you feel happy, sad, or other emotions.

Shadow work is discovery work. It dis-covers or uncovers inconsistencies in the personality as it reveals what is different about your personal truth than what has been told to you by others. Personality is part of who you are. It receives input from others and registers that information as what you think you believe. Shadow work is not about changing the discrepancies you find. It is about noticing falsehoods in the personality and allowing your deepest truth to emerge.

Duality or contrast may increase during the exploration. Do not give up your self-discovery process when old limiting patterns are in conflict with your inner truth. Breakthrough will come as you get to know and accept yourself. Your new beliefs will redefine what you believe and will positively affect the way you treat yourself. You will have broken the codes that limited the expression of your personal truth.

Personality

The right side of the triangle represents personality, also referred to as the ego, shadow side, psyche, inner child, and such. Personality is necessary for an Earth experience. Without personality we would all act and think the same way. There would be no diversity in the way we express ourselves or the way we experience life on Earth.

Within the first seven years of life, the personality begins to view itself as separate from Source and others. Ego is often viewed as a separate or evil entity that needs to be removed, eradicated, or harshly disciplined. Ego's desires and curiosity naturally partners with the body to freely explore and have experiences. Ironically, ego that has adopted erroneous beliefs also causes us to despise or mistreat our body, seeing it as carnal flesh that needs to be punished and brought into submission. The body does not take sides with Spirit or personality. It is constantly trying to reset and restore itself from the mixed messages our programming imposes upon it.

Personality always desires to be loved unconditionally. It starts a perpetual and endless Search for Home but does not know what it is searching for. We feel we are missing something. So, we try to be a better person or to not feel things that we were taught to be undesirable. Repressing our feelings, we begin condemning ourselves, hating our bodies, and judging our experiences. This conflict of interests creates a stressful inner dialogue that tries to sabotage the unification process.

When the personality is not allowed to explore and experience life as the third part of the system of wholeness, emotional experiences are judged and shut down. People may try to overcome or remove the ego/personality, thinking it is demonic or evil. This indicates a strong belief in separation from Source. There is no need to battle anything that has forgotten its true identity. We do need to understand the difference between our personality when it is Spirit-driven and when it is program-driven.

Things we are taught or that happen to us in childhood create programs or imprints that mold our way of approaching our adult life. In general, people in our day and age tend to live in a constant state of fear in their struggle for survival. The human psyche or personality is able to deal with stress; in fact, some of it can even be useful. When there is an event that is bigger than our ability to process the accompanying emotions, the inner child may go "out of body" or into an illusory state in order to cope. The work we do with this part of our psyche is valuable for integrating the original experience, so we no longer need to be triggered by people and circumstances. The reason we are triggered is because this inner child (personality) is asking the adult self (Spirit) to help it come back into present moment awareness and integrate the emotional charge that the original event(s) created.

We cannot get back to Soul until we work with the wholistic system without being drawn back into the dramas of Earth life. How do we do this? By returning to our innate curiosity. Through exploration, we allow the physical body to process, move, and have experiences without judgment.

"As you honor authentic thoughts and emotions within, you actually start the process of healing automatically. Your work is to allow healthy flow of authenticity and to seek new perspective and strength of connection with Life."

~ Jamye Price, October 2015 Light Blast Newsletter

Body

At the bottom of the triangle is the body, which communicates by neurological routing through its entire system, both in a spiritual way as well as in a physical way. The body has a natural mechanism for coping when one is not strong enough to deal with the truth. Routing is pure physics.

The brain receives signals from Spirit and personality. Confused by opposing instructions from Spirit and the misguided personality, the body may manifest dis-ease. We do not trust the body because we have been programmed to believe that something is wrong and must be fixed. Fortunately, the body knows how to self-adjust. It can go through extreme circumstances and still be able to function.

As we begin to sense and feel without judging the experience, we bring the sensory part of the physiology together. We create a new baseline at the foundation of the triangle.

"There is no judgment with God. The God who created you out of love, placed a piece of itself into you called a soul – and loves this soul as itself."

~ Kryon through Lee Carroll

Spirit, body, and personality are part of the whole Concept. Subcategories have to do with personality or programming resulting from experiences we have on Earth. There are an unlimited number of subcategories. Anything can be framed as a subcategory for the purpose of exploration and discovering what is similar and different, what is aligned with personality and what is aligned with Spirit.

We are looking for what is good and working well in a subcategory and what is hindering our evolution. As we harmonize or integrate duality, the subcategories will fall away, and we will move back into the oneness of the Concept. In other words, as humans collectively move into a higher stream of consciousness the human condition will improve. Be aware though—things could get worse before they start to get better. Tearing down an old building makes a mess. Once the dust clears the new creation will appear. Be patient and stay in your still-point as much as you possibly can. Hold your vibration and love yourself unconditionally. Comfort the part of you that feels scared as things shift.

Trauma is usually associated with a huge upsetting event such as war, loss of a loved one, divorce, financial loss, rape, robbery, or a hurtful relationship with a spouse. But what is traumatic to one person may just be an annoyance to another. Honor your sensitivity. Pain is a subcategory. It does not randomly show up in our lives for no reason. It serves a purpose. It is a sign that something in our body needs our attention. If some part of your body feels a little out of whack, explore what it is saying. Your response to your body or emotions is a hands-on discovery piece that works the tri-vector system.

Bridges that connect personality with Spirit and body are formed when we realize that we carry the entire unification program within our own three-part system. We need the password or code to access the advanced program. We begin to recognize what we had to learn in order to fit in and then start accepting and trusting that our innate curiosity has always been available to us.

Experiencing Physical Embodiment

There is a fun way to work with the psyche to integrate a traumatic experience. We know that repressing it does not make it go away. Complete resolution or integration means you are less likely to get triggered by people and circumstances that remind you of the original incident or trauma. There are many ways you can integrate energy, shift patterns, and come to a place of peace with your past.

Gregg Braden shared a YouTube video titled "The Ancient Technique to Making Tough Decisions" from which I paraphrased the following paragraph:

"In 1991, scientists made a discovery that every human heart has 40,000 or so brain-like cells that creates a neural network in the heart. These cells think independently of the cranial brain. Every experience we have registers in both the brain in the head and the brain cells in the heart. The brain is a polarity organ—left and right hemispheres—and if you ask your brain a question when you are stressed, it will go through logical, analytical, and past-event loops that keep you from getting a clear answer. If we try to heal trauma using only our thoughts or brain, the healing will not feel complete."

The Reset Breath© was introduced publicly in 1994 into Quiet Miracles, a non-profit program created by Brenda Julian Williams. At that time, there was no real science that could prove it worked. Those who were experiencing and using it just knew that it did. In order to change any pattern, it is necessary to first signal/alert the body/brain that a change is coming. The Reset Breath© sends that signal and reminds the body and brain to move in resonance with all systems. It also provides a quick, effective way to focus your attention on the communication going on within the body and your personal 18 inches. It allows the body to notice, pause, notice again, reset, and self-adjust simply by bringing awareness to the exhale. Sounds like a lot going on and yet it all happens within a nano-second. That is the human design.

When we find our thoughts contradicting our inner truth, or when we face an emotional dilemma, it helps to stop for a moment and use RBQT-18" to bask in the quietness of "Home".

> Many breathwork practices have certain counts to begin to bring the in-breath and out-breath into a more resonant balance. This gives us an opportunity to return to our individual, natural rhythm. While those practices require that we commit to a time and place to begin, The Reset Breath© encourages us to continue to live in the ever-changing vibration fields that we already move in. It asks that we do so with conscious awareness. Meaning you are aware of your surroundings as you move through the day. Each time you find yourself sensing or noticing something that distracts your focus, you pause and reset. With practice, the behavior changes and the reset occurs naturally and organically. That is, after all, how we were originally designed.
>
> ~ A Wholistic Concept developed by Brenda Julian Williams

In addition to the Reset Breath©, you may also connect your three-part system with the use of Quiet Touch. The recognition of the human body's ability to self-regulate, balance, and create its own healing, along with the knowledge that occasionally it needs some gentle assistance to guide it into action, is the basis for Quiet Touch.

In early development, humans had to learn to manage emotions. Emotion is unique to our human experience upon Planet Earth. Some sentient beings do not experience emotion. Education and childhood experiences create programs or emotional imprints that mold the way we approach relationships and situations in adult life. When you get triggered as an adult, this is your inner child asking your adult self to help him or her come into present moment awareness and integrate the emotional charge that the original event(s) created. When bringing fragments of the soul back into wholeness after a trauma, it is important to be in the body and to feel all that is arising.

Sentience is the essence of who you are—your soul signature. The heart is the seat of the soul. Sentience is located in the heart area of the human body. This command center for sentience expands outward to the electro-magnetic field around the body. The energy in our cylindrical 18 inches of personal space is all we are required to manage. That sounds easy enough, right? Because the soul uses the personality to anchor itself to physical reality, the personality/ego also has access to the heart command center. The soul views the world through ego and pretends to be human in order to experience life from a lower perspective, clouded by limiting filters and programs.

In the Body, Not Out of It

Most of us find it easier to maintain our energy field when no one is influencing us, but it is important to be able to access that flow when life is happening right in front of us. Here is an exercise to help you get into your body anytime you are feeling anxious or fearful. Try this type of meditation for a few days and notice what changes.

Find a private space that is your go-to spot where you are not likely to be interrupted by others. You may have multiple places where you go to be alone. Set your intention to simply have an experience without attaching to outcomes. The idea is to be fully aware of and present with all your sensory abilities.

Physical Feeling

Keep your eyes open and do one Reset Breath©. Engage with your body and your senses. Do you feel any difference after one breath?

With awareness and attention, gently place your left palm on your chest and find the spot where the energy is strongest. What do you notice about this "sweet spot"?

Now, place your right palm on your lower abdomen. Do you feel hot or cold? Do any emotions arise? What thoughts are brought up? Have a sense of curiosity without judging what comes up. Just tap in and feel.

Energy Feeling

Put your palms together in front of your body. Feel energy pulsating and moving between them as you gently pull your hands away from one another to about three inches. Move the hands together with palms almost touching. Then, gently move them apart to about six inches. Move them in toward one another and feel. Slowly move them apart and feel the buoyant energy expand to follow your palms.

- What do you notice when you hold your hands together and move them apart?

- What word would you use to describe the sensation you experience in this space?

Continue to feel the energy from your electro-magnetic field—your personal 18 inches that surrounds your body like a cylinder of light. The top of the cylinder is open to the cosmos. The bottom of the cylinder is open to Gaia. We are energetic by nature and therefore connected with Mother Earth. Mother is never stagnant nor locked into one frequency. She is always in flux. Her baseline consistently flows between 7.83 and 8 Hertz to help the human body remain in the movement of the planet. Known as the Schumann resonance, it is the frequency of the original form. The resonance is affected by the emotional quotients of human behavior. It allows for individual human growth and takes into consideration the wide range of frequencies that flow within the collective field of humanity. When doing the exercises offered in this book, you are connecting to Earth's natural flow of 7.83 Hertz.

Move your hands slowly around inside your personal space. Engage deeply and feel the flow of energy. Notice any shifts in your emotions as you move energy in the space around your body. Can you describe what you feel?

With arms stretched out in front of your body and palms facing you, notice what you feel in your hands.

- Do you feel your energy pulsing outward from your body to your palms?

- Do you feel any external energy on the backs of your hands?

- Allow yourself to go deep and feel it all.

Hearing

Tune in to your space. Listen to your breath. We are not trying to hear the voice of guidance right now. Listen for the silence in the zero-point field. Have your thoughts settled down?

Listen to the sounds around you. If there is a movement or a sudden noise around you, does it distract you? If so, reset to where you were before the interruption.

Seeing

Pay attention to pictures that form in your mind. Look at nature or things in the room around you. Try to maintain the sensation of discovery in your body and environment without getting distracted by what you see.

Smelling

Notice any odors or aromas in the space around you. Smell your own scent. Are you able to smell energy? Keep discovering the feeling and connection of your personal cylinder of energy.

Tasting

Is there drink or food in your space? Sip or taste it. Chew on something. Taste the salt on your skin. Are you still feeling the stillness and peace as strongly as before?

Engage with all your senses and explore for as long as you wish. This is the connection of the Spirit, body, and personality that helps you recognize your wholeness. Use this technique to self-adjust and explore your own energy and body.

When there is flow in your three-part system, you will naturally embody more Spirit. You will be in tune with your physical body. You will better understand the personality's desire to explore, create, and express. You are learning how to be and accept who you. You are learning to sustain your own vibrational field while living in a changing and unpredictable world.

CHAPTER 4 ~ What and Where Is Home?

As we became entrained to outside influences, we began to rely on what we were told, shown, and thought we knew. This programming taught us to deny our needs and desires in order to please others or to be liked or accepted by someone in authority. To stay physically and emotionally safe, we may have modified our response to life in order to stay on somebody's good side. We may have learned to manipulate to get what we want. The ascension or homecoming is a stripping away of this façade and recognizing that it is okay to be who you truly are. As we grow in spirit, we notice that what we were told, shown, and believed is often inaccurate. We are spirit in human form having an experience with a programmable personality always seeking Home.

What is the sacred space that we call Home, and how might we recognize it? As I mentioned in the previous chapter, "In the beginning" is the zero-point field in which all movement occurs—where Source is in an undifferentiated state before becoming geometric fractals of light called spirits or souls. When Spirit is in physical form, Home is not a location but rather a state of being where Spirit, form, and personality operate in concert with one another and the environment. When you feel your connection and participation in this stillness, the illusion of separation falls away. Yet you know that without you, and your piece of the puzzle, the beginning is missing one of its children. You sense your importance and self-worth without arrogance.

When you live as though you are separate, the longing for Home becomes a mind construct as you think about how to get there. Going into the still-point does not require thought. It just is. Like in the Wizard of Oz, Home is a constant and our entire vibrational field can experience it by simply being in the stillness. It is not about doing anything. It is about allowing yourself to be fully and physically immersed in the moment—the now—not then, when, or there. We do not reference who we were yesterday. We are new every day. We express different parts of our personality each day and from one setting or circumstance to the next.

When the still-point is reached, it expands your entire vibrational field, and your energy field becomes a safe space to be your true self. Here, you may feel energy throughout your body—especially around your heart, head, and solar plexus—the very places we shut down in order to be accepted by others. Where do you feel Home in your being?

To get into the intimate depths of our knowing, we access the space between what we know now and what is yet possible to be experienced. As our perception changes from a viewpoint of lack ("What am I missing?") to a curious wonder ("What else of God's creation can I experience?"), we see the beauty and precision with which all things are created. Some things will be of interest to us, and some things will not. There is always a choice. That is the beauty of diversity and individuality. In this moment, we are an integral and connected part of all that exists. Feel that!

The 6th Element

Our biggest (and perhaps most important) mission is to consistently allow Spirit to merge with the physical body and allow the curious personality to explore. This aligns the three parts of wholeness with the 5th Element of Unconditional Love, which propels us toward the unified 6th Element—All That Is.

When Spirit, body, and personality have fully united with one another and aligned with the 5th Element of Unconditional Love, the crystalline light body will be complete. We will step out whole and complete with all our systems working as they were designed.

The tri-vector system is constantly working in a wholistic way to bring us to the 6th Element:

- Soul is directing spirit
- Spirit is working with the body and personality
- Personality is curiously exploring as it looks for Home

Change is something humans do not like very much, and yet it occurs all the time. We are not the same as we were ten years ago or even one year ago. Through uncertainty, we are urged to walk by faith and not by sight. The Coronavirus pandemic caused an already fragile concept of life to become even more unstable and our future even more uncertain. This global event can be seen as a catalyst for helping us move into all that we are and can be. Old ways that kept us stuck in detrimental world systems are being dismantled. Something new and better is emerging. I encourage you to trust the collective homecoming process and your own movement within this time of change. The change that we create for ourselves can be fun! Build your trust and believe that all your needs will always be met.

To reach unification, your intention must not be encumbered by your desire to see a particular outcome. You may think things need to be a certain way, but the divine has its own idea of how the ascension should go. Life is not a competition. Do not worry if someone is ahead of or behind you in their journey to wholeness. Everyone will get to where they need to be when they need to be there. Practice daily surrender to divine will and you will have peace in the midst of the shifting of paradigms. The key to consciousness is curiosity. The password is courage and the willingness to persevere. If seeking allows for curiosity and exploration, it moves all parts toward wholeness.

When you are moving to a new level or vibration, your discomfort could be indicating that shift. Your body may be using discomfort to let you know it is transmuting or releasing an old energy pattern. Try not to assume there is something wrong. From the still-point of your inner being, you will instinctively know when or if you need to see a doctor or a healer.

> "The vagus system, or ventral vagus complex, provides insight into the importance of listening to our 'gut feelings,' which are often ignored. Its sensory capabilities monitor the external environment and the internal body systems."

> ~ Brenda Julian Williams

We integrate mentally, with mental constructs. We have been using mental constructs as building material rather than concepts, which are all-encompassing. We embody wholistically through vibration or feelings that works with the entire system of Spirit, form/body, and personality. Not the brain, but the heart and the gut.

Feel the vibrations used for guidance and assimilation by working with the three sides of the triangle. When you have an inner conflict, or feel fearful, or sense resistance to change, stop for a moment and curiously explore your response to a few questions below, which involves the personality while moving the body into feeling the vibration of an experience. Spirit is directing this movement to help you determine where the roadblocks are.

- What do I notice in my body? Is there movement or stagnation?
- How does my body feel?
- What am I experiencing emotionally?
- What is going on in my personal vortex?
- Does my self-talk show compassion toward my body or emotions?
- How much love and care am I giving my body?
- Does my response to this discomfort come across as self-judgment?
- Am I integrating an energy download?
- Do I need more sleep, exercise, food, or water to support my body?
- Is my concern with this experience relevant at this point, or do I need to remove my mental attention from it and feel what is arising?
- Have I felt this way or addressed this situation before? How do I navigate this differently now?

You are at a different place now than you were the last time you faced a similar situation. You are perceiving things differently. Even if you take a similar route toward resolution, you can avoid potholes this time because you are smarter now. You are not likely to make the same missteps because you are functioning differently in your body. Remember, there is no pass or fail. Life is not a test—it is an exploration!

I use light language in my day-to-day life to interact with my personality and keep Spirit in the driver's seat. Taking light language to the next level wonderfully supports the three-part system. Therefore, I use light language as part of my reset practice. As I lay my hand gently upon my heart and do the exhale, inhale, exhale, I softly and lovingly speak light language to myself. It amplifies and stirs energy in my personal space. This allows me to keenly feel the presence of Spirit in my body. My emotions may respond with joy, tears, peace, or empowerment. I let myself explore and feel these sensations. I know something has shifted for me when my body and my emotions are alive with a new feeling.

I realize that not everyone has activated their verbal light language, and some do not wish to. That is fine. Everyone can use or benefit from the Reset Breath©, Quiet Touch, and 18-inch field process (RBQT-18").

Light language is telepathically communicated through the senses and inner knowing. I can speak light language and others can understand it by feeling it. If we cannot communicate in a practical way, we get stalled. The question becomes, how can we use it practically when light language is not literally translatable into words? How do we take this unknown language to Walmart and get someone to understand vibration? We take what we know and filter it into experience. To me, that involves having fun and being creative.

I use the Walmart example because I have heard a lot of healers talk about how bad the energy is there. I do not go shopping to experience everyone else's energy. My interaction with the world is not about getting anyone to agree with me or live the same way I do. I go to the store to pick up the merchandise I need and to anchor codes. I am a lighthouse. Naturally, I shine! I consciously transmit energy because I desire to be a blessing. Those who can receive the signals Spirit transmits through me will be positively affected.

If I sing or speak light language in public, then it is an authentic expression of the love pouring from my heart, or because I am energetically reminding someone that my personal field is sacred and not to be infiltrated. No one gets to syphon my energy remotely or in person. My empathic abilities let me know if my boundaries are being challenged.

Like someone who whistles down the aisles in the grocery store, I need not apologize for being happy or explain what my "song" means. The light of my Spirit does not need to be hidden, nor does my ego need to draw attention to itself. Together, my body, Spirit, and personality are experiencing each moment and integrating wherever I go.

Directives, Distractions, and Detours

Most of us aim to live by the Original Directives and be fully present as we walk hand-in-hand or heart-to-heart with Spirit. We are often tempted to be distracted from that intimate relationship. Distractions take our focus off what is good right now and instead show us what was bad about the past or what could be upsetting about the future.

Our culture teaches us to judge ourselves and others as we struggle to conform to unattainable standards. We place more value on education, performance, appearance, and status than we do in developing our intimate connection with Source. We worry about how we look and what we must do to survive. Materialism, prestige and status, job performance, peer pressure, comparing our unique expression with the "norm" and modifying who we are to meet those expectations—these also distract us.

Frequencies generated by cell towers, satellites, radio waves, and the collective human consciousness can distort your ability to discern your way. Electronic devices that should remind us of our connection with Source and one another have actually done the opposite. They have caused people to live in a virtual reality and to ignore those right in front of us. They are so distracted by technology that they are not in touch with what they truly feel and what is truly going on with their body or emotions. There has been experimentation with implanting a digital chip within the human brain, thereby wirelessly connecting the brain to a computer to accelerate learning. How much of ourselves are we willing to give away to a machine? If we do not wake up, we may become human robots with artificial intelligence. I say this to emphasize the importance of feeling and being fully present. The technology we have in our world today is reverse-engineered or copied from the natural and biological abilities we have a Spirit in human form. Our sound and light code connections have been hijacked. Fortunately, the work we are doing with our cosmic guides is restoring our divine routing in the body. When we are fully aligned with Spirit and free of vibrational distortions we will not need devices to accomplish the communication that is natural to the divine human.

Even spirituality can be a distraction. We do much of our meditation and spiritual practices from a place of distortion. The minute our body or personality begins to shift we start wondering if we are doing it right. We are concerned about what people are saying about us. Even in group settings where the energy is moving, we feel embarrassed if we start crying, laughing, or shaking in response. A lot of my clients feel incomplete because they are not doing their mission. They do not realize that their mission is not about doing anything spiritual. It is about letting Spirit be our closest companion—so close that we can trust and follow our inner guidance because our personality is learning to walk in sync with Spirit. This is true surrender.

Materials and tools should be used to enhance our inner work. I have known people to spend mega-amounts of money on stones, crystals, candles, and all sorts of magical tools. The Bible never mentioned Jesus pulling a trailer behind his donkey to carry his miracle-working paraphernalia. I have a few drums, wands, staves, crystal skulls, singing bowls, statues, art pieces, musical instruments, smudge sticks, candles, incense . . . Wow! I still have a bunch of stuff even after giving away some when I moved from Sweethome. I enjoy these tools, but I do not depend upon them like I once did. Now, I see them as training wheels. They helped me learn to work with energy before I had confidence to trust that Spirit within me was enough to get the job done. We do not need a bunch of physical tools to work the Tri-Vector System™. Everyone has the resources within to move through the unification process.

The world does a good job of making us feel small. Believing that you are less than someone else or less than divine will prevent you from living to your full potential. Relationships, self-judgment, and past experiences can also become distractions. When we are fearful of other people's judgment, or we judge others, we block the flow of Source energy.

Those of us on our journey Home have spent much of our adult life unlearning what we were taught in childhood. But when we become obsessed with the past or projecting our attention into the future, we are not present in the here and now. Much of the past is a reiteration of lies that distract us from realizing our divine power and true self-worth. I have worked with clients who are consistently on a fault-seeking journey to unearth some ancestral imprint, alien implant, or past life wound they believe is dragging them down. The only thing that is dragging us down about the past is the power we give it over our current experience. We have enough to deal with in the here and now. But what about doing our shadow work? Shadow work is not an excavation that needs to take up all our time. Whatever is ready to be resolved will present itself through the personality. We do not have to go looking for it.

> Shadow work is healthy. We need to be able to swim
> to the depths of our darkness to find what we need
> to heal. However, the longer you stay in that
> darkness the easier it becomes to lose sight of the
> light inside you. Work with your darkness, but do not
> let it swallow your light."
>
> ~ hbbbiofeedback on Instagram

Lack of positive focus on the here and now is an age-old problem. When Jesus took the apostles Peter, James, and John up the mountain, they had no idea what they were in for. Jesus started to shine with bright rays of light. Moses and Elijah appeared and started talking to Jesus. Pretty unusual, I would say. But, instead of being curious and fully experiencing the magical moment, the apostles suggested they put up a worship facility for each of the glowing light beings. What they did not realize is that the temple was already inside them. Then, a voice spoke from a cloud. That was too much. The men fell to the ground in fear. That event would be outside my rather large comfort zone as well! The Bible does not say whether the men were ever treated for PTSD, but that is likely why our cosmic companions do not materialize in front of us very often these days.

If distractions go too far, they become detours. I have experienced both and I am sure you have too. It is good to know that we can always come back into resonance and find our path again. It is through the choices we make every day, all day.

Who is in charge of your life most of the time? Spirit or personality? It can be difficult to tell sometimes. For example, let's look at scarcity versus abundance.

From an ego standpoint we may believe that the world is indebted to us and that we should have everything we want regardless of how it affects others. People are willing to walk all over one another to grab the last roll of toilet paper off the store shelves. And when there is lack, we blame God or the Law of Attraction or whomever we think is at fault. This view is demanding and ungrateful. We perceive lack when our heart is not in alignment with Spirit. This is a perfect example of when the personality/ego is ruling the roost.

On the other hand, we know that there is an abundance of unlimited supplies in Source—more than enough to meet all our needs and bless others. And we know that Source wants us to live a joyful, abundant, and fulfilled life. When we come from a place of gratitude and heart-felt trust for Source, the scarcity mindset of the ego does not take precedence. Even when we need to economize, it becomes a game in which we look for bargains, or we reduce, reuse, repurpose, and recycle. We ask for what we need and stay in gratitude as we watch things we need come into our reach. It amazes me how much we can actually do without and how little it actually takes to live a simple life.

The following story of Elijah and the Widow at Zarephath (1 Kings 17:7-16) reminds me of the miracles that occur when we trust that our needs will be supplied.

Sometime later the brook dried up because there had been no rain in the land. Then the word of the Lord came to him: "Go at once to Zarephath in the region of Sidon and stay there. I have directed a widow there to supply you with food." So he went to Zarephath. When he came to the town gate, a widow was there gathering sticks. He called to her and asked, "Would you bring me a little water in a jar so I may have a drink?" As she was going to get it, he called, "And bring me, please, a piece of bread."

"As surely as the Lord your God lives," she replied, "I don't have any bread—only a handful of flour in a jar and a little olive oil in a jug. I am gathering a few sticks to take home and make a meal for myself and my son, that we may eat it—and die."

Elijah said to her, "Don't be afraid. Go home and do as you have said. But first make a small loaf of bread for me from what you have and bring it to me, and then make something for yourself and your son. For this is what the Lord, the God of Israel, says: 'The jar of flour will not be used up and the jug of oil will not run dry until the day the Lord sends rain on the land.'"

She went away and did as Elijah had told her. So there was food every day for Elijah and for the woman and her family. For the jar of flour was not used up and the jug of oil did not run dry, in keeping with the word of the Lord spoken by Elijah.

The prophet Elijah (a celestial shaman) received and acted upon clear instruction from his inner guidance (God). Even when faced with the widow's doubt and despair he stood strong in his belief that God would provide for him. He was not concerned with the widow's religious beliefs—it seems apparent that she did not worship the same God as Elijah. Nor did he try to change her beliefs; she could still cook a meal for herself and her son and die if she so chose. Elijah's faith that the flour and oil would not run out stirred confidence in the widow. Either she hoped that Elijah was right and her needs would be met, or she had surrendered her ego and realized that one more meal was not going to keep her or her son from dying.

"Consider the lilies, they don't toil nor spin
And there's not a king with more splendor than them.
Consider the sparrows, they don't plant nor sow,
But they're fed by the Master who watches them grow.

We have a Heavenly Father above
With eyes so full of mercy and a heart full of love.
He really cares when Your head is bowed low.
Consider the lilies and then you will know."

~ Joel Hemphill

Celestial shamans cannot effectively do our work while doubting whether or not the Universe is going to provide for us. In a crisis, we get creative and find alternative ways to meet our needs. I trust that if my service is no longer needed here on Earth, my body will die or ascend into a light body, and my spirit will go Home. I also know that my body will not die until divine will allows it. If I contract CoVID-19 and recover from it, that is divine will for me. Fear will not direct my decisions. Having said that, I am doing my part to stay well—I still have work to do on this planet. Therefore, I will continue to practice good hygiene and stay home like I have for many years.

Shape-shifting and non-resistance are the means to navigate your personal path in a world that is radically shifting. If a mask is required to go into a store to purchase needed supplies, then I will wear a mask that has my energy and vibration embedded into it. I set my intention that I am playing a game or performing the role of a character incognito. I do not like the connotation that covering the mouth symbolizes or that black masks are worn in satanic rituals. We still have freedom of speech. I speak light language in the store, and no one can see my lips moving as I anchor and restore light and sound codes!

I have been asking Spirit to come fully into my awareness and operate through me more and more. My desire is to have my first response to any fear that arises come from a practice where Spirit is in control and the personality is observing. I have noticed the answer to that prayer being answered in everyday experiences and synchronicity that provide practical blessings and lessons.

I was vacuuming the hallway right before sitting down to work on this book today. The rubber anti-slip mat was barely peeking out from under the rug I had tossed into the carpeted hallway when I mopped the bathroom. The vacuum cleaner caught the edge of the rubber mat and started whining and gagging. I frantically reached for the power button after not being able to pull hard enough to release the mat that was going deeper into the abyss. I could not find the power switch on the machine. That frustrated my personality, which quickly spewed four-letter words that evolved persons are not supposed to utter. Yeah, right! After I found the switch, I started complaining about the way the vacuum cleaner manufacturer had installed the power button underneath the hoses where I could not see it or feel it. I could barely reach it without getting on the floor. Suddenly, I realized my personality was in the driver's seat. I started laughing. It was like watching myself as a cartoon character—a maniac coyote chasing Road Runner over the cliff in slow motion . . . Pause . . . Gasp! . . . Drop! . . . Beep, beep!

"Ooh, Miss Ego, you are having a moment. I sense you enjoyed that release of emotional energy. Now I am going to put some loving Holy Spirit on you and help you find an alternate way to express yourself." I spoke in light language for a minute, then in English. "How about some gratitude, Miss Ego? I am thankful for my vacuum cleaner. The mat getting caught in the beater bar did not break a thing. Everything still works well! I am thankful for my house and the physical stamina to clean it. Thank you, body, for being so strong. These rugs are nice, and the mats do a great job of keeping them in place. I enjoy my life and I am grateful for everything I have created—including an ego that reminds me to be thankful when things do not go the way I think they should."

When you have crazy thoughts or an emotional outburst, you may think you have an entity attachment. This is proof that our guidance is distorted. Many of our thoughts are filled with nonsense and serve only to distract us from our focus of allowing Spirit to be the first responder. Thoughts are background noise coming from the frequencies of collective chaos being broadcast from beings that are not aligned with the Original Directives. Harmful or disturbing thoughts are not your thoughts unless you choose to own them. They are not from your spirit, but you can use their energy for your own benefit.

Sometimes there is a message worth discovering. How do you discern the message your thoughts are projecting? Only give attention to the thoughts that get your attention. If a thought makes you curious, there could be something to explore. You will know by asking yourself, "Where is the gift in this?" You may be stressed, tired, hungry, or worrying about something that happened last week. You might also ask, "Is this helping to create a happy future or positive mindset right now?" If it is not, stop and reset before you move on. Do not get distracted with overanalyzing. Acknowledge the behavior that was out of alignment. Express gratitude for the experience. Know that any time you have an unpleasant thought or emotional response, you also have the opportunity to explore it and decide what to do about it. Stay curious, my friend!

If we do not engage with the mental chatter, we are less likely to get caught in the web of lies we hear in our heads. Repetition and focus create habit; the more attention you pay to misaligned thoughts, the stronger they will get. It is like they are saying, "Oh, she wants to play with us. We will give her more toys." Then next thing you know your head is filled with more crazy thoughts and you get worried or scared, which serves to further amplify that energy and provide proof that something must be "wrong." No wonder it feels like a possession. You have given away your power.

If your field is erratic right now, it is time to stop what you are doing and deal with it. Do not wait until next week. There is no need to call somebody else to fix it for you. It is okay to feel angry, just do not project that anger onto another person. Reset your system and you will be able to navigate smoothly through the challenges that are surfacing. The sooner you get into the practice of dealing with stuff when it shows up, the less baggage you will drag around with you. Soon it will become natural to take a pause and get back on track.

Every time you release something, you activate something and vice versa. Energy is always moving and looking to fill space. As you resolve the energy of a painful experience or past trauma, you are filling yourself with (activating) new knowledge. Explore and get curious about the rhythm, energy, and vibration of who you are becoming. Recognize your safety, your abilities, your strength, and your freedom.

The clearer we get today, the better we can navigate the enormous challenges the planet is going to be faced with. I hold a very positive picture of our future, whether we continue to abide on Earth or in another dimension. Groups, countries, and races are uniting in prayer with one voice and loving intention to initiate proactive changes that will benefit everyone. This will open the way to divine Intervention of the Christ Consciousness. I do not know whether there will be a rapturing of souls in which we are escorted on lightships to a place that Christ has prepared for us. This current planet Earth is being flooded with more unconditional love and light than ever before. I do expect miraculous events to unfold as old systems and structures collapse. I see improved social living conditions emerging as a result of major changes in the global economy unparalleled to what we have seen before. A more balanced distribution of wealth and power will flow as governments, politics, military services, medical practices, and financial institutions work together to share commercial and natural resources. The lack of materialism and greed will be apparent as loving communities unite for the good of all. Our spiritual and telepathic gifts are already opening, and we are seeing miracles coming from our own prayers and hands. In future generations, our bodies will evolve from physical carbon density into crystalline light bodies.

We knew before our incarnation to the Earth plane that there would be great opportunity for soul expansion during which humans could transition from the state of collective amnesia to a full recollection of our divine authentic nature. We currently live in a magnificent time where the collective humanity is shifting in awareness as energetic attachment to lower energies are being severed. These cords on the lower vibrational spectrum of polarity have been holding humanity back for eons. These lower energies are felt by all as they arise. Some people are reluctant to change and let go of familiar dysfunction. Therefore, the collective is experiencing significant difficulties, turmoil, anxieties, and challenges which impact some more directly than others. I have been incredibly blessed throughout my life. Some of these blessings are results of actions I have taken. Others are due to circumstances I did not control. There will be some things none of us can control. But there is much we can do even if we witness more turbulent periods of challenges over the next few years. Keep your focus on the big picture even as you contemplate and process a wide variety of feelings. All of this change is leading humanity to lasting peace and happiness. Divine purpose is being fulfilled.

Most lightworkers I speak with have a peacefulness about it all. We have the skillsets within own field to flow above the chaos. We can do this by moving into the silence and allowing our inner wisdom to work without the brain getting involved. The brain is connected to the path that we have used in the past. I believe that is why light language is so useful—it bypasses the analytical brain and activates tri-vector movement to rescript detrimental codes back into alignment with your divine matrix codes that correspond to the Original Directives.

We have the understanding on how to reset or self-adjust whatever we question or is out of resonance. When you take a moment to move back into the physiological experience of sympathetic-parasympathetic balance, the body immediately clicks into the still-point and begins processing within a matter of seconds.

CHAPTER 5 ~ What Does a Celestial Shaman Do?

Starseeds, empaths, shamans—all lightworkers—feel drawn to helping others. That outward expression is secondary to the main reason any of us is on the planet—to unify Spirit, body, and personality. This is something we must do for ourselves. No one else can do it for us.

Our personal evolution does have an effect upon the collective. We are in this together and individually. As we invite Spirit to come more fully into our body and we surrender our ego, we send vibrations into the world that help others find their way Home. In fact, the more we are aligned with divine love and holy compassion, the more easily we are able to help others. Your service to others is a natural byproduct of living in a unified field. It will not matter what occupation you choose to provide income.

Sometimes we get stalled in our evolution and we seek help from healing practitioners. While celestial shamans are not here to save the entire world and fix everything for everyone, we can assist one another to embody Spirit, evolve the personality, and shift the body into light.

The typical work of a shaman may include soul retrieval, releasing attachments, repatterning detrimental energy in the psyche, offering emotional support, repairing subtle bodies, opening and balancing chakras, managing energy, and activating and transmitting codes. Some celestial shamans are able to assist people with integrating the energy of a walk-in and helping the body adjust to new frequencies. Some read and "re-script" Akashic records to override imprints/anomalies of past life trauma.

Celestial shamans are connected with star groups, planetary systems, and multiple star races. Getting quiet and "feeling" is a better way to connect than sitting with the expectation to hear or see your guides or get something from them. When you can feel them around you or in your body, it is much more meaningful. Then, it becomes a relationship rather than a one-way guidance. In my experience, we are our guides and they/we are not separate. The team is me. I am them. Thus, the "Me-We" team. The more we are in touch with our feelings and our body, the more we will sense this loving and unified presence.

Every celestial shaman with feet on the ground has a vibrational team that is uniquely assigned to them. Each team is made up of ones from the multiverse who are part of the Earth ascension project. Not all members of the multiverse were invited to participate in this project, and others were asked to leave because their agenda did not align with the Original Directives. The agreement is to not create anymore discord on or interference from this planet because it is affecting the entire multiverse. Our teams are doing and revealing whatever is necessary to aid in this.

A lot of people have no clue about what their team is doing. Or they are struggling because their team does not have the desire and Source agreement to clear anomalies. Thus, things go awry, and the practitioner succumbs to distractions due to distortions and interference in their personal field.

In the vibrational field that we hold for others, celestial shamans may use light language, hand mudras, written symbols, or sounds to download and activate codes that rewrite energy patterns stuck on loop in the body's brain and mental records of the personality. They direct energy in a powerful way that positively affects and transmutes energy imprints in the body, emotions, and DNA.

Sometimes when I am working with a client using the languages of light, I get images and a sense of what is being done for the client. I can see the technicians working on the physical body and imprinted patterns in the personality. I might hear the technicians say something like, "We are updating communication modules and devices that are obsolete." I see team members removing things from the client's body or putting electronic-like devices into the body. I am told that these devices upgrade the communication system, rewire the brain and/or neural pathways, and recalibrates resonance with higher spectrums of light. Thus, spirituality and physicality come into agreement.

Cosmic technicians are from many multiverses, but in the early days many systems were monitored by the Andromedans. It would happen during our sleep. The body would need recovery time and put us in bed with what felt like an illness. Some would be completely down for a day due to intense pain as things were being changed around. These effects have been referred to as "ascension symptoms." I do not usually notice much difference in my energy during a planetary event, moon phase, or celestial alignment. But when we moved through the Lion's Gate this past August, I had some intense emotions come up. My skin felt tingly and itching like it was crawling off my body. I slept for ten to twelve hours at night and took naps during the day. I was not motivated to do anything but sit in my recliner wrapped in a blanket watch gardening shows on TV! I learned that many lightworkers were feeling similarly.

Everyone on the planet is influenced by the alterations that have been adversely done to the DNA template or set of genetic instructions that our bodies are designed to follow. The body continues to draw instructions from this template, which includes the body's ability to reset itself. Tampering has been done to our DNA through food sources, environmental toxins, viruses, vaccinations, medications, negative alien implants, abductions, and frequency bands emitted from electronics and the bandwidths (especially 5G) that support them. These make the body subject to sickness, aging, and death. Our star teams and cosmic allies are reprogramming these detrimental agents which will allow the physiology to return to following its original blueprint design. Thus, we will be able to receive photon/plasma light and hold higher vibrations and frequencies in the human body and shift our consciousness.

Many of you reading this are practicing shamanism or feel very connected to other worlds or dimensions. You may be doing some or all the things mentioned here. You may have begun to speak unknown languages, see codes or symbols, direct energy with your hands/mind, or feel as though you are in two places at once. You may be getting downloads, integrating soul aspects, and have more loving expression toward yourself and others. You may also be clearing detrimental patterns from your life experiences and those of your family line.

New ways to work with energy are being revealed as we become able to handle the higher frequencies. Currently, celestial shamans may work with their team to do any, all, or more than the following:

- Activate Spiritual Gifts
- Anchor Codes in the Grids
- Channel Frequencies from Higher Fields of Consciousness
- Clear Energy Infiltration
- Empower Self and Others to Live Authentically
- Resolve Patterns in Subtle and Physical Bodies
- Integrate Spirit into the Body
- Journey Interdimensionally
- Open and Close Portals or Star Gates
- Perform Etheric Surgery
- Provide Physical Healing
- Remove Implants and Imprints
- Receive and Transmit Codes
- Retrieve and Integrate Soul Aspects
- Re-script Akashic Records
- Interact with Lightships
- Sense Guidance through Empathic Intuition
- Shift Humanity out of the Old Paradigm
- Exchange Information with Off-Planet Teammates

I will not go into detail about each one of these, but I will examine a few of the tasks that I have been most involved with over the years. Unlimited miracles may occur through us; therefore, this list and my exploration here cannot cover or predict the wonderful ways your gifts may unfold.

Journeying, Portals, and Gates

Journeying into the underworld on behalf of another person can also be known as intercession, bearing the burdens of another, or setting captives free. Shamans may journey or intercede for someone who asks directly, or they may respond to their cosmic team asking them to work with energy grids, a specific country, community, or race of people. Many are urged to transmit light codes for a world event, the wellbeing of animals, or nature/elements in general.

The journey may offer the shaman some pertinent information or reveal a shape, sound, symbol, or code that represents a doorway to freedom from illusion. These codes can open and activate codes in our human DNA. Sharing these codes with a client or the collective human field can be beneficial. I have been directed to post light codes on social media, my website, or in my newsletters. I trust that the person(s) who needs the energy download will connect with the posting as it is sent into the ethers.

Some celestial shamans collaborate with high-vibrational beings in cosmic sectors that have specific duties such as opening and closing portals on Earth and in the bandwidths around Earth. Advanced cosmic beings hold geometric passcodes that allow celestial shamans to move through stargates to specific timeline coordinates or zones on the grid network. Some of the codes we write in light language or see in our spiritual eyes are maps and coordinates that show the way to or from these gates and dimensions. Portals are also used to interface with our teammates. Through these portals, we may receive downloads, travel to lightships or other dimensions, or visit our parallel counterparts to assist them with their ascension or homecoming. They may also visit us.

Timelines are not linear. They are dimensions in which parallel or simultaneous lifetimes or realities take place. Dimensions could be located inside the vibrational rings or concentric circles of consciousness around the Earth. Multidimensional aspects of our soul can travel or live in other realities while we are only aware of ourselves in one incarnation. As stronger light waves come to Earth, we are beginning to feel that we are in more than one place at a time. I have been in group gatherings where the energy was so strong that the entire group realized they were in another dimension.

The physical body is a representation of the cosmos and vice versa. Everything "out there" is also "in here" (inside the body) because the body is a cosmic portal though which Spirit is connected to Source and the body. As above (in the cosmos) so below (in the body). The light body, inhabited by Spirit, has access to multidimensional realities where we exist as soul aspects or diverse spirit expressions of Source.

A vector or triad wave is designed to begin a cycle and come back in three different ways. When the vector signal is sent through a gateway, such as the nervous system of the body, it assesses everything while allowing one to choose what to do with it. Since this feedback bypasses the primitive brain, either your Spirit makes the decision to release energetic glitches that are discovered in the blueprint of a dimensional field, or your personality decides to hold onto the misaligned energy. It depends upon who is in the driver's seat of the personality. If Spirit decides to rectify the anomaly, the personality may change as a result. You might have clarity on issues that were once puzzling, the body may heal, you may find it easier to forgive, and your emotions may be calmer. Realigning with the divine template for unity changes our station of identity or vibrational placement on the fabric of space/time.

If there are gates in the cosmos and the human body, there must be gates on Earth. Places where UFOs are often sighted, and planes and ships disappear have strange magnetic variances that draw missiles off course and pull meteorites out of the sky. The Bermuda Triangle, Mexico's Zone of Silence, an ancient doorway carved into a rock wall in Peru's Puerta de Hayu Marka and other mysterious places are said to be a portal to other worlds. There are several places on Earth with unusual rock structures and hieroglyphics thought to have been created by advanced ancient civilizations. Some shamans feel called to live or work in particular areas due to portals that exist there. At times light grid workers are asked to help open or anchor portals in a location.

The personality is housed within the physical heart space which is connected to unlimited dimensions of reality. Shattered or holographic parts of the personality may become stuck in other dimensions during astral travel, out-of-body or near-death experiences, or during trauma in which the personality is dissociated. This detour into the denser vibrational realms can come as a result of decisions made by a rebellious ego or that of another misaligned personality. Entrapment or "binding" is can generated by words and actions that intend harm to another person. I have seen fragmented parts of the personality bound in a dense state of consciousness through curses, rituals, abuse, or maleficent intention. I have used light language to release such geometric codes.

Some portals are controlled by those who attempt to sabotage the Original Directives of the multiverse agreement. Mythology mentions characters who have traveled to the Underworld. The Bible refers to the entry of this portal as "The Gates of Hell." Jesus was said to have entered this dimension and set captives free after he was crucified. Celestial shamans may need to enter this zone in order to rescue a fragmented personality that has been energetically bound there.

Some portals were opened years ago and are no longer needed or in the correct place as civilizations come and go, or the Earth orbits around the sun. Celestial shamans can open portals to allow increased rays of light to come to the Earth to help with the ascension of human consciousness. The sun is doing much of this work for us.

Celestial shamans move from one dimension to another consciously and subconsciously. When this occurs during dreamtime, one may awaken feeling like they have been working all night. People have often mentioned seeing me in their dreams during which I was speaking light language to them or giving them instruction. This "night work" is an example of how we travel to other dimensions to assist others. I have encountered aspects of myself and my guides in animal forms during my dreams. This is an example of how we can be in more than one place at a time.

> "Can you really be in two or three places at the same time? Yes, you can. You'd better get used to it. It is all part of the unthinkable—the unseeable. Perhaps the you in the mirror is also a part of another's energy? If you understand that, then you are well on your way to understanding how you are all part of the orchestra on an interdimensional Lattice . . . yet

all are pieces of God. The Lattice sings a beautiful tune—a tune of harmony—a tune of love. It is a tune with a message that tells all of you that you are eternal and interconnected."

~ Kryon through Lee Carroll, The You in the Mirror

When we learn to work with energy and re-master our thoughts we realize we are unlimited. We may be able to transform our carbon-based physical body into a lighter density that can travel with us. This ability to teleport is mentioned in the Bible in accounts of Jesus, Elijah, Enoch, and others. Philip disappeared as the Spirit of the Lord "suddenly took Philip away" after baptizing the eunuch. Philip then appeared at Azotus (Acts 8:39 – 41).

The less density or duality we choose to experience, the higher light quotient we can hold in our body and personality. The more light we emanate, the less discord and drama we will want to create. When we show unconditional love for ourselves, we will naturally love others more. We love others as we love ourselves.

Retrieving and Integrating Fragments

Fragments? As in shards, parts, and pieces? Yes. As multidimensional beings and individuations of the Divine Cosmic Intelligence, the embodying spirit has multiple counterparts or aspects residing in dimensions besides this Earth plane. Any of these parts can influence or assist us in our life on Earth. We can also assist and influence them.

Like a computer file can slip out of place (defrag), parts of the personality can fragment or scatter during severe trauma or if emotional overload occurs. An aspect of our personality may "flee the scene" or dissociate during the ordeal and go into hiding in an alternate reality until it feels safe to return or until you call is back. Anytime we experience a similar or disturbing event, an aspect may pop up with a message or reminder that we have fragmented files, parts, and pieces that need to be re-integrated.

Personality fragments can be recalled, cleared of karmic imprints, and reunited with the embodied Spirit. This practice has been known as soul retrieval. Reintegrating these aspects is an important part of the ascension process, or returning to wholeness.

The best way to retrieve a fragmented aspect and integrate it is to realize that the part has not actually gone anywhere. It is a repressed emotion held as an energetic imprint in the emotional body. It may be felt in the cells of the body as pain or illness. It affects the mental field and causes us to judge, withdraw/shut down, and feel everyone else's stuff but our own. It carries a magnetic ability to attract people who also believe they have similar wounds.

When we encounter an unpleasant thought, person, or situation, we need to stop before things get out of hand. We tend to keep plowing through an upset and ignore the feelings arising inside. Rather than putting your emotions on a shelf to deal with later, pause and reset. Feel your personal energy cylinder/tube with your palms facing you. Check for infiltration.

- Do you feel a heaviness, pulsing, or other sensation on your palms?
- What do you feel on the outside of your hands?
- Do you feel your energy pushing out from your heart space?

- Is someone's energy, or the group field, pushing into your space?
- Feel whatever you feel and notice the shift in how you feel.

When you reclaim your personal energy space you will feel calmer, lighter, or buoyant and back in sync. By clearing your personal tube, you reduce the number of triggers that keep coming up over and over. Triggers are messages that a repressed emotion or personality part is trying to get your attention. It needs to be felt and acknowledged in order to be integrated. This is best done at a causal level. If we only work on the mental level, we repeat the story, deepening the imprint in the neural pathway without bringing resolution. Every incident based upon the signature of the original trauma can be processed and brought into present awareness. I find this type of work is more effective by adding light language because it speeds up the process and helps hold the vibration of the new pattern. Light language not only uses mapping coordination codes to locate trauma where it is stored, it creates a vector and offers a space for you to shift your perspective.

Working with Entities and Attachments

Celestial shamans are like spiritual midwives. We may assist souls who are coming into a physical body on Earth–either as a newborn baby or as a walk-in soul taking up the mission where a former soul left off. In the case of the latter, we work with our team and the guides of the departing spirit to resolve residual energy imprints or karmic debts not resolved during a person's previous incarnation(s).

You may be called to work with clients who have attachments or entities. It may help you work more confidently if you know that what we call an "attachment" may be an energy structure—such as energy imprints and astral debris—rather than a presence seeking resolution from a past event/lifetime.

The Spirit cannot return Home to the 6th Element until the personality is completely integrated or unified throughout all the dimensions of Earth. The Spirit departing an expired body may move to a higher dimension of light and live separately from the unresolved personality energy that is stored in the astral body. This energy may be seen as a projection or plasma-like apparition by people (especially mediums). Due to frequency incompatibility, low-vibrational patterns do not exist in higher dimensions. That would compromise or change the frequency of those dimensions. Each dimension holds its own frequency as a supportive structure for our work and exploration. Whatever is forgiven in the lower bandwidths of Earth is also forgiven in higher dimensions. A personality can join with the Spirit in the afterlife when resolution or forgiveness is offered.

Personality is always seeking Home and it knows this is done through incarnation and unification with Spirit in a body—any body. Astral energies may confuse your light for the tunnel of light (portal) that a Spirit uses to make an exit to higher dimensions. Astral bodies and ego personalities have come to me many times in my life. I am sure many of you have dealt with astral entities clinging to your electromagnetic field. It can feel like a possession or like you are going crazy when this happens. This is because in addition to trying to bring our own personality into submission, these "hitchhikers" are siphoning our energy.

In my book Whose Stuff is This?, I mentioned working with archangels to help clear the departed without having to consciously work with each entity. When my then-husband and I first moved to Sweethome we not only had to put the fixer-upper house back together, we had to deal with a lot of hostile energy leftover from the former owners, who engaged in drug and alcohol abuse. One member of the family had died in a fatal car crash and was buried on the property. Even though that corpse had been exhumed before the house went on the market, the astral energy could still be felt by those who were energy sensitive. We cleared a lot during the first year and things got much better.

I had opened a portal of light to access various dimensions for intercession and shamanic work that we were doing during our workshops. There was a loving presence in the chapel that many empaths could feel even before walking in. I would meditate, pray, and record light language transmissions to keep the portal clear and pristine. When I went to the chapel alone, astral personalities would be drawn to the portal because they wanted to cross into a higher dimension in the "between lives." I tried to ignore them since the archangels had been doing such a good job of preventing entities from hanging out in my personal field, but something had changed. My team now needed my involvement again. I was the team member with feet on the ground, and they wanted to show me a new technique for dealing with the "deceased."

It was during this time that I became aware that astral visitors could not move into higher dimensions without having a reunion of their fragmented parts. I began using light language to clear karma, retrieve fragments of the personality, offer forgiveness, transmute dense energy patterns, and loosen geometric codes that held them bound to lower realms. After this recalibration, I visualized putting the parts and pieces back together and crossing the reconstructed "package" into a higher dimension that it could now resonate with.

I would notice a difference in my field after this process, but I wondered how often I was going to have to do this retrieval and integration routine to keep the unwanted energy at bay. Like training wheels on a bike, the practice served as a starting point for the work that would soon become automatic. I was instructed to create a portal that would serve as a holding place where astral debris and parts would wait for me to come "stir the waters," so to speak. With each crossing-over routine, I gained confident in the work. The routine got easier and the energy shifted faster as I was able to cross multiple souls at one time. Soon, my intention took over the job of having to visualize the collection, clearing, and reassembling of fragmented parts. Anytime I felt the urge to "flush" the energy that had accumulated in the chapel portal, I would set the intention that the portal would open, and the process would occur without my babysitting it.

There is a good reason Catholics pray for the deceased souls to be released from purgatory (dense levels of reality). Evolution of the personality continues in the space between lifetimes. We can support one another with our prayers regardless of whether the personality is in a body or in a dimension in the afterlife. Celestial Shamans have the tools to help disincarnates resolve karma and send the ego/personality aspects into a higher dimension of light to join with the corresponding Spirit.

An attachment could be one of your soul aspects coming Home from a mission ready to be integrated. An attachment can be an energy construct created from a belief system or fearful thought form. Many attachments automatically clear when they are properly acknowledged as feelings or emotions. In my client sessions, we transmute or change the energetic frequency of the attachment using drumming, light language, compassion, and affirmation.

Attachments can be transferred from one family member to another. Some negative attachments transfer from a perpetrator to a victim during abuse. Known as familiar spirits, these energy patterns may be passed down the ancestral line. When you intimately know and feel your own energy, you will stop allowing yourself to be a victim. You will take appropriate action without hesitation.

Not all entities are negative. Some observe as an apprentice when they are ready to reincarnate. Perhaps they are evaluating your life to see if Earth life is in their best interest. You may or may not be aware of their presence, but they are usually harmless. A "deceased" ancestor may attach to your field and serve as one of your guides. Depending upon their level of personal evolution, the guidance they offer may or may not be beneficial.

Attachments can be cleared by calling upon your guides and angels. Ask them to gather all parts and pieces of the personality and clear the karma (leftover energy patterns) and help the Earthbound personality integrate with Spirit in the lighter realms.

Intercessory Birthing

Celestial shamans can personally experience and activate massive energy shifts in others. We may birth nonphysical energies such as codes, events, walk-ins, life changes, clearing of karma, or manifesting creations. Like a woman in labor, this task may be felt in the body and emotions. It is not usually painful, but the energy can be so intense that it knocks you flat for a few minutes or even hours. Men can give birth too, as can women who do not have reproductive organs. Groaning, crying, or heavy breathing are natural responses to this kind of energy flowing through your system. You might birth for others as if you were a surrogate for them. You may also birth things for yourself or the world.

A birthing can be a release from an old condition or habit. I have seen people cough, spit, or have dry heaves during intense movement of energy. People have vomited when being delivered of an addiction. Writhing on the floor, making animal sounds, crying, feeling physical sensations of giving birth, jerking, groaning, shaking, speaking unknown languages, and other responses are not unusual in delivery sessions. However, liberation of this type is not typically welcomed in a church service. Fear and the need to maintain control of one's reputation prevents a lot of releases that could take place. I have decided not to quench the Holy Spirit, or judge what people experience when vector energy is activated in a physical body. I have experienced intense energy and know why some people are afraid of it.

At an inner-city gathering in 1999, I was shaken like a rag doll by an energy that I could not control. My body bounced up and down like a rabbit for about five minutes and I thought I would pass out. Then, as strangely as it started, the energy lifted, leaving me feeling tired, but fine. Mostly, I was confused. What was that? The proof of any spiritual experience is in the pudding, so I looked to the outcome of what had just transpired. I felt like I had been born anew. I had courage and emotional fortitude. My walk-in occurred within the next few months, bringing with it some big changes in my life.

This type of birthing is like a hard reboot of your three-part system. It is normal for the body to feel sleepy or tired after being overcome with intense energy. Rest and take care of your vessel while you integrate the energy and experience. If a birthing seems to be going for a long time, or if the energy feels stuck, call on another intercessor or celestial shaman to assist you with singing or speaking light codes.

Amy Carroll related a story to me of how she was to birth starseeds before she could integrate her full aspect of Divine Mother/Father. The following are her words:

> "My heart space portal opened and I "birthed" the following beings into this realm: Arcturian alliance here for on-planetary ascension process (some will be in bodies and some are not), elves and the angelic souls that are to be embodied here for this process. There were tools/gifts that came through as well to equip these beings.
>
> This process was a very odd sensation for me. It started as uterine pains like birth pains but instead of moving down, they moved UP into my heart chakra and I could feel the energetic equivalent of the portal expanding and a baby sliding out. At one point, it felt like people walking through a doorway, with some lingering like hesitation but then I could feel them come through. At another point, gifts were birthed through the throat chakra (speaking their truth, being heard by others on the mission, etc.).
>
> These newly-birthed beings are going into physical bodies and waking those who have not woken up to their galactic origins. Those who are awake are activating their latent gifts and pretty much giving them the call to service, the urgency to use those gifts.

We do not have to do clearing for others if they are able to do it for themselves. I do not want others to become dependent upon me or look to me as their guru. The goal is to get people to do their own work once they can feel their connection with Source. However, there are some people who are so stuck in their pain that they cannot clear themselves. You can put a plate of food in front of someone but if their arms are tied they cannot pick up the fork. Celestial shamans may clear a path for another person so they can begin to find their way. While I do not suggest taking other people's energy into your body, you may be triggered to empathically feel when some unresolved pain is being released. When I feel an emotion coming on suddenly, it is a signal that I am starting to intercede or birth. The sensation leaves once the work is complete.

Transducing and Transmuting

We are bringing in high frequency energy and simultaneously transducing it really fast. We cannot plug a computer or coffeemaker directly into an overhead powerline down the street. The voltage is too high to be used for household appliances but is necessary for carrying and distributing the current over distances. In North America, this raw electricity must be stepped down or transduced into a current that can be tapped into at a 120-v or 220-v receptacle.

Much like an adult bird chews up a worm and makes it more digestible for its babies, it is important for celestial shamans to create a resonate field that allows for easier energy integration.

I had a client whose light language was activated in class while holding the hand of her yoga instructor, who was speaking cosmic languages and did not know she was a celestial shaman. The young woman got such a high influx of cosmic energy it nearly blew the routing of her nervous system. Her body had been shaking involuntarily for days when she called me. The first thing I did was use light language to transduce or step the energy down into a current that she could actually plug into. Then, I raised the vibration of her body to match a frequency that she was able to integrate. Within minutes, she stopped shaking and felt calm.

As humans have an electromagnetic body, those who are consciously "plugged in" to their cosmic source may be energy distributors, transducers, and conductors. Celestial shamans who hold a high vibration are serving as modern-day pyramids, powerlines, and cell towers. We are receivers of telepathic messages or frequencies coming from cosmic realms, the sun, or lightships within the circles of Earth. While receiving downloads and sharing light language with others, my body has responded with jerking, vibrating, hearing buzzing or high-pitched sounds, and feeling all kinds of physical or emotional sensations. We take in "high voltage" energy and step it down into a useable current that the population can handle. Then we direct the frequencies of these downloads and deposit them into the Earth grids or collective field of human consciousness where others can access the assistance these codes provide.

The clearer channel we are, the more high-frequency energy or light quotient we can handle and hold. What constitutes a clear and pure channel? One who is mastering a state of non-judgment, who is living in the present moment, who feels and lovingly deals with whatever comes up, and has neutralized detrimental experiences of childhood. In other words, they have awakened to Spirit and started stepping outside of the imprinting/programming of material reality.

Anchoring Light Codes

Have you ever been driving along and wondered, How could I have missed my exit? I have traveled this way many times. How did I get here? I do not remember getting off the interstate.

After countless experiences like this I finally realized that Spirit was leading me to a coordinate on the grid where I was to anchor light codes on Earth. These days, I no longer question it; in fact, I allow extra time in my travels in case Spirit decides to send me on one of these "adventures."

Latitude and longitude help us identify locations on the Earth. There are many more finer points that establish a mesh or energy network. Those who work with the Earth's grids are aware that the connected intersections are aligned with points in the cosmos or the grids around the Earth. When we anchor light codes, we are depositing frequencies at strategic points on the light grid.

How do you deposit codes? The same way we do everything—we use our intuition and intention. We ask Spirit, "Does this anchoring need a ceremony or tools, or is my presence in this place enough?" Ceremony and ritual are powerful because they focus energy and draw your attention to the work. In my celestial shaman weekend workshops at Sweethome, Spirit instructed me to have my students walk through the woods with their written codes on a sheet of paper and anchor light codes as directed from their spirit team. We used only light language for this exercise. No English words. If you want to try this and your languages have not yet come through, you may sing, hum, tone, whistle, click, make animal sounds, etc. to keep your mental body from imposing its will upon the process. If you choose to walk in silence, use a breathing technique that keeps your focus in the present moment.

You can use your intention, prayers, and light language to deposit codes wherever you are. Sometimes the cosmic beings deposit codes into the Earth and we are asked to show up at a certain place and time to access them. There is a repository of light codes in the grids of the Earth.

Brenda and some friends were called to Pilot Mountain in North Carolina in 1997. There is a big rock at the top of this little mountain. The rock has four sections. Each person tried different points on the rock until they felt they were sitting on the specific piece that called to them. They were then downloaded with a Ray of Holy Compassion that was being grounded and broadcasted at Pilot Mountain that day.

Like the human understanding and expression of love, our compassion contains conditions and is only shared with those we feel deserve it. This Ray of Holy Compassion is about having compassion for those who have not earned it. This type of compassion allows other people to have a journey unlike our own in the way that they need to have it. We are not to interfere with it or judge it.

I have had clients who are in a really uncomfortable condition due to their unconscious creation with ego having too much control. My role is to lead people to find their inner teacher. My coaching style is a self-evolved modality that includes doing shadow/inner child work, clearing limiting beliefs, integrating life experiences, and empowering by recognizing and expressing your authentic self. Still, it is difficult to watch someone "hit a wall" that is part of their learning. I can comfort them, help them clean the wound, and put a bandage on it. But I cannot "heal" them. Healing carries the connotation that something is wrong and needs to be fixed. I can offer them tools to help them integrate and recognize their wholeness. Rather than trying to heal someone, I want Spirit and that person's teammates to do the work in/through them. Using the codes of light language, I transmit the blue triangle which offers the opportunity to transmute past experiences to a neutral point. From there the pathway to freedom becomes clear.

In the victim-perpetrator dynamic of the old paradigm, it is difficult for our personality to have compassion for those who do not live up to our expectations. That does not mean that people get to walk all over us and harm us with their dysfunctional behavior. Boundaries are an expressed part of compassion. It is not helpful to you or a person with ego in the driver's seat when you enable them or try to make their life easy by circumventing their consequences. We can choose to avoid a person whose ego is in charge. And, when we do have to be around someone who is ignoring Spirit's prompting for realignment, we do not have to take on their energy or lower our own vibration. If you cannot love them in person, love them from afar.

Hardship is a matter of perspective and how your nervous system responses to harsh conditions. Those who are in an abusive relationship sometimes feel that their abuser is the more powerful one. The truth is your standing in your personal power feels like a threat to the abuser. Some people allow themselves to be beaten down to the point of not wanting to live before they realize they have the power to change their lives. Change and loss are some of the deepest ways in which life helps you evolve.

One client I worked with was in an abusive marriage for about ten years. She was often told that she was stupid, and nobody wanted her, or that she would never amount to anything. Before she met this man she was extremely outgoing and vivacious. Soon after being told these lies, she wanted to fade into the background. The resolving of these beliefs is a process that takes commitment to re-parenting yourself with unconditional love. It is good to be your own best friend and intimately feel your grief and sorrow as well as your joy and power.

As a celestial shaman it is important to stop believing that you are less than someone else. You may have been persecuted for being different or having spiritual gifts. As a result, some are afraid to use their creative power to make their lives enjoyable. We are being called to step into authenticity and let our light be seen.

CHAPTER 6 ~ Light Codes, the Keys to the Kingdom

"I will give you the keys of the kingdom of heaven; whatever you bind on Earth will be bound in heaven, and whatever you loose on Earth will be loosed in heaven."

~ Matthew 16:19

Light codes are the instructions that consciousness and creation instinctively follow. They are to creation (including the human physiology) what binary codes are to a computer. Codes instruct programs and applications in an electronic device to perform a function. Light codes speak to all of nature, the DNA, the physical and subtle bodies, the electromagnetic field, the personality, and everything in the multiverse. They communicate on an energetic or quantum level and provide divine instructions to realign divine matrix patterns that have been distorted.

Because the codes of light are frequency and vibration, they are valid in any universe or dimension that we can access. You do not have to micromanage the light language transmissions you send out. You can set an intention to allow the energy to go where it needs to and do divine will.

The tri-vector wave contains multiverse intelligence. Do not worry about how the waves are received or what they need to do.

Every electronic device operates by following instructions or program codes running in the background. They are like the parasympathetic nervous system of the human bio-computer that controls our heartbeat, breathing, digestion, and other involuntary functions. We do not have to think about how a computer works in order to type an email. We do not have to be an electrician to use a microwave.

Containing the codes of light and vector movement, the Keys to the Kingdom can be used for binding and loosening, opening and closing. If a stargate is shut, its access is restricted. Only those with the passcode (gatekeepers) can go through it. Opening portals is a form of loosening. If a personality is out of alignment with the Original Directives, it is bound or stuck. Loosening sets the personality free of detrimental programming. Celestial shamans are cosmic ambassadors sent to heal the brokenhearted, set the captives free, and loosen those who are bound.

> "The Spirit of the Lord God is upon me; because the Lord hath anointed me to preach good tidings unto the meek; he hath sent me to bind up the brokenhearted, to proclaim liberty to the captives, and the opening of the prison to them that are bound."
>
> ~ Isaiah 61:1

As a form of surrender to higher love, we can also bind/connect our personality to Spirit as indicated in the Lord's prayer. I have added italics to show how the Keys to the Kingdom are used in this prayer led by Jesus in Matthew 6:9.

"Our Father in heaven, hallowed be Your name (surrender is both binding and loosening). Your kingdom come, Your will be done (binding human will to divine will) on Earth (the planet and within us) as it is in heaven (6th Element/Home). Give us this day our daily bread, and forgive us (set us free from) our debts as we also have forgiven our debtors (set others free). And lead us not into temptation (distractions and detours) but deliver (loosen) us from evil (anything not aligned with Original Directives)."

"There is another, more ancient language, more conducive to discourse on this level, but you have forgotten it. It is the universal language of light. Its transfer of information is accomplished through the actual projection of living informational units. These units are at once more specific and more inclusive than your words. They have been designed to convey organic information of concise, yet comprehensive, informational content. Simultaneously with this conceptual communication, you are subliminally receiving this same information through this living language of light, though your preoccupation with words leaves you with no awareness of it at this time period."

~ Ken Carey, The Starseed Transmissions

Many people have started visibly seeing geometric codes in water, nature, objects, clouds, and in the air space all around them. This ability to see energy often starts in the dream time where the encoded languages of creation are easily heard or spoken.

As a Key to the Kingdom, light language was designed to connect us with Spirit and work the tri-vector system as one continuous perpetual motion. It helps to keep the movement between Spirit, body, and personality constantly in motion. The language helps Spirit to download into the body. It increases the ability of the body to house and hold the vibration of Spirit, and it serves as a bridge to help the personality trust Spirit and surrender to change.

The language of light contains the codes for creation and does not depend upon our ability to mentally understand what we are sending or receiving. It bypasses known/learned languages that keep our focus on the mental plane. It brings us to the zero-point field or still-point that calms our thoughts and focuses on inner vibrational frequencies and felt sensations.

The beautiful thing about light codes is that they instinctively know what you need at any given moment. Light codes analyze anomalies that are present when they move as vector energy through a field. They find your point of need and shift whatever is ready to be transformed. A transmission of light codes may mean something different for one person than it does for another. Codes are like stem cells, which differentiate by following genetic instructions. Each cell knows what type of cell it needs to become—a heart cell, eye cell, skin cell, bone cell, etc.—in order to form the whole body. The Keys to the Kingdom know when to bind and when to loosen.

Light language is beneficial in every way to a shaman who works in multiple dimensions. It is a fun and powerful form of telepathic communication that inspires a childlike love for self and others. Children know the language of light. Many are shut down from speaking it by adults who do not understand the value of play. In my light language activation workshops, I make it fun to feel like a child again. I ask everyone to share what led them to the workshop. This helps each person to settle in and feel safe in the group setting. Then I ask them to make sounds—just vibrate and play around with the voice. This is so hard for some who have been shamed or shut down and feel that their voices are not good enough to be heard. When we compare ourselves to others and harshly judge ourselves, it quenches the flow of creativity. I offer an opportunity for every participant to activate and speak, sign, gesture, and write light language in their unique way of expressing.

We all operate with individual codes that are part of the multiversal codes. You may have noticed how different light languages sound, and how varied the symbols look. You and I look different and yet we are all part of the human race and a unique aspect of Source. Vibrational resonance and matrix plans draw people to one another. We may resonate more with some light languages or written codes than with others.

The best way to understand the codes of creation is to look at the technology we have on Earth: computers and peripherals, binary instructions, coding languages, applications, programming, hardware and software, cloud storage, satellites, space stations, live streaming, memory, Internet, cyberspace, sending and receiving messages across time and space, operating systems, files and downloads, monitoring, defragging, updates and upgrades, wireless networks, smart phones and tables, motherboards, firewalls and virus protection, hackers and malicious programs—the list goes on. They are showing us how the spirit world works. Movies, cartoons, and video games speak to the fact that humans truly desire, or wish it to be possible, to have abilities beyond what we are currently able to perform. Hollywood sparks our imagination to accept things as real that have formerly only been part of our imagination.

People ask me, "Where do light codes come from? Who are you channeling?" That is like asking, "Where does the Internet come from?" Most of us do not question where cyberspace is or how it works. Very few ask what company provides the internet service to my house. We trust technology and use electronic devices, but few understand the coded languages that tell the device how to interface with the human user.

The signals, sound waves, frequencies, bandwidths, and codes of light are from the multiverse, which is Source—our Home. That is why light language feels familiar and touches deep parts of our soul. But some codes are channeled from cosmic beings who helped to create the template for the human body. Some of these beings are working on upgrades that remove anomalies and help lighten the density of the body, creating a light body structure. These Beloveds are part of our celestial teams. During client sessions, I can feel the energy change when one of my guides or a guide from my client begins to tone or vibrate through me. It feels like I am plugging into a celestial mainframe and downloading codes that are specific for that person.

Another question many of my light language class participants ask is, "Is light language the same as tongues?" The basic cosmic language I use now is the same as when I first activated the gift in 1994. Even though the church I was attending did not use the gifts of the Spirit, I had been asking God for the gift of speaking in tongues. I had it in my mind that I was going to be a missionary in a foreign country and that I would be able to speak and understand the language of the people I would be sent to without having to learn the language the old-fashioned way. That did not happen. I am not a missionary imparting religious doctrine to any country, but I am a celestial ambassador to Earth, a place that does seem foreign at times.

The cosmic languages I speak continue to develop and expand to include more bandwidth and faster download speed. When love is the primary motivator for all we do, the anointing will increase and get stronger. Our true power is love. Opening our heart to our higher self allows more love, honesty, and transparency in our daily experiences. Surrendering to divine will becomes easier when we graciously accept and share the love that naturally flows from Source.

> "If I could speak all the languages of Earth and of angels, but did not love others, I would only be a noisy gong or a clanging cymbal."

> ~ I Corinthians 13:1

Many people have had hurtful experiences with organized religion. Since there are rules and expectations for what is acceptable during a church service, the use of tongues has been controversial or even prohibited. Spirit and personality want to experience freely and with curiosity. When spirit-filled people speak in tongues there may be physical shaking, unusual sounds, or playful antics. This response to energy movement may disrupt an orthodox service, and some would say that is ego. I am not here to determine whether another person's experience is valid. The same shaking, crying, laughing, and unbridled sounds in one of my light language workshops would be as normal as apple pie.

So, it is a matter of respect. If cosmic tongues spoken in a church meeting is not appreciated, then perhaps it would be best to select another place to express it. Trust your own knowing and live in freedom as Source blesses you in surprising ways.

Every experience we encounter on Earth is recorded in the Akashic records. Celestial shamans are able to overwrite virus codes contained in the records of Earth experiences. These are not the same records as the intergalactic records, which log the travels/positions of all our soul parts in all dimensions throughout the multiverse. The intergalactic records are the history journals or logbooks with the maps, coordinates, and codes of our interstellar travels. They also serve as tracking devices to help us connect with our soul aspects in parallel lives. When you begin to function as a multidimensional being you will notice how you can shift from one parallel life to another on any given day. You may or may not remember what you did while on your journey, much the same as when you awake and have no memory of your dreams.

To effectively perform the role of a celestial shaman, it is important for you to be in your body and aware of your feelings. Recalling past lives can sometimes be a distraction from what is going on in this lifetime and what is happening right now. You are in this body to enjoy the life that you have here and to participate with all who show up as part of your story. That said, I also believe that we affect and are affected by our soul aspects in simultaneous lifetimes. If I am working with a client who is seeking to resolve a troubling pattern, I will ask questions and use light language to trace the pattern back its origin. Most of the time the pattern began in the childhood of their current life, but I have seen the roots go back to a past/parallel life. Our goal is the same—to integrate or neutralize the energetic signature of the initial infraction and all experiences resulting from it.

Light codes that carry vector movement can be felt as they find distortions and realign them to the divine matrix codes intended for wellbeing and synchronistic meeting points. When people listen to my light language or meditate on codes I've drawn for them, they have an opening, clearing, or shift in energy depending upon what they need at the moment. This is where light codes differ from medicines which have a chemical formula with instructions for doing a specific thing. Medications have no regard for how they may upset other parts or systems of the body. Have you ever noticed how drug commercials list more side effects than they do benefits? Light codes are living instructions concerned with the well-being of all systems. Their main objective is to remove glitches, restore function, and unify the body, Spirit, and personality so it may return to Home.

Using codes such as the language of light, celestial shamans have the ability to reprogram and activate dormant DNA. Light codes transmit instructional downloads that can repair, update, and upgrade the operating system of the human body or experience. It knows exactly what to fix in every device, body, and situation in order to bring it into alignment with a higher ideal. These codes are an effective way to work with the level of conscious awareness in the collective field as well as each persona or psyche. Each individual is confronted with the decision of which operating system to run. One is based in fear, the other in love.

As mentioned earlier, I have incorporated some of Brenda Williams' material in this book. The sharing of that material began at a local Starbucks, where Brenda and I had our first in-person meeting in years. Our energy was out the roof that day, and I knew I would be overwhelmed if I did not quickly settle into my still-point. I took a Reset Breath© and silently spoke light language as I consciously felt my body touching the chair. It dropped into my knowing that I was getting downloads from Brenda even though I did not understand much of the scientific information she was offering. My experience has taught me that this kind of encoded AirDrop of information will make sense later when I know what questions to ask. So, from the still-point in my Spirit I listened without trying to put anything into context while receiving. I followed her energetically and telepathically. A smile warmed my face and heart as I relaxed and saw the humor of our interaction.

One of my gifts is being able to put into understandable language the vast concepts and overviews that Brenda distributes like a tornado touching down in multiple dimensions. Our partnership is unique, and I love it!

Technology from Non-Physical Realms

Some of my discoveries came while integrating the codes that were downloaded during a celestial shaman workshop that Amy Carroll and I co-facilitated in May 2019. Both of us were shown a model of how our current technology is a primitive representation of how things work in spiritual realms.

Much like a biological computer, the human body is able to receive and transmit codes or frequencies. Electronic devices need to recharge and periodically receive upgrades to the operating system, during which we have to power down and stop using the device. The same is true for our body and energetic system. It needs to be reset from time to time. If you are not getting enough rest and you keep pushing to accomplish mechanical repetitive things that you do not resonate with, your body will give you a warning signal. Some people call it sickness or discomfort. I call it "having an upgrade." The coronavirus has forced the masses to pause for a sacred moment and get in touch with what is really important in our human experience.

During a recent drum circle one person saw and felt themselves as a pyramid. Just a few weeks earlier I had watched a YouTube video about the Pyramids of Egypt—not those we typically hear about that served as burial or resurrection chambers for kings and pharaohs, but the original pyramids. Based on vector mathematical structures of 3 6 9, the pyramids were built on Earth's equator and 30° latitudinal lines and in alignment with certain celestial locations that emit primal interval tones from our universe: perfect unison (1:1), perfect octave (2:1), perfect fifth (3:2), and perfect fourth (4:3). The geometric codes in the structure of the original pyramids allowed them to conduct, receive, or transmit wireless energy. They were believed to emit frequencies or energy from the cosmos to the Earth similar to the way satellites and 3G, 4G, and 5G waves send signals in our day and time. Human bones, organs, and tissues can hold the energetic or soul signatures of a person. If a body is mummified and placed inside the pyramids, the energy of that person could continue to be transmitted long after death. Some even believed that the energy of the pyramids could resurrect the bodies of the ones buried inside. The valley of dry bones in chapter 37 of the Book of Ezekiel seems to give credence to this belief.

Many people I speak with feel a connection to ancient Egypt. I believe the reason for this is because we had lifetimes there during which we toned, spoke, and deposited ascension codes that could be used to help transform human consciousness at the completion of the 25,920-year cycle that we are now in. We may have been the ones who inscribed symbols on walls of caves, tombs, stone structures and in the healing chambers or pyramids. Celestial shamans may be the ancestors of the mummies in the desert caves. Who knows? We could be the temple priestesses and dancers who are now reactivating the codes of heart-centered spirit alignment.

The ancient pyramids may have served as devices that act upon human consciousness. The technology known as 5G was intended to distort the communication network within the body and destroy human DNA, causing illness and death. Starseeds holding higher frequencies who are working with their galactic team are reducing the harmful impact and alchemizing the frequencies into ones that raise our consciousness and restore divine DNA. Can you see why our most important "mission" is to maintain a positive attitude of gratitude? Be available to follow your inner guidance at all times.

"You intended to harm me, but God intended it for good to accomplish what is now being done, the saving of many lives."

~ Genesis 50:20

Since our DNA carries the geometries and codes of the pyramids, we are reminded that when we tone, write, gesture, or speak the codes of light, we are using sound frequencies, mathematical vectors, and geometric symbols to call forth the codes that we deposited in ancient times.

The Blue Morphogenic Screen

Many people have done work with the Akashic records. I have never felt drawn to have a past life regression, but I know it can be helpful to learn how an experience with someone in your current life might be related to something that happened in a past or parallel life. As we interact with various components of our consciousness on the time-space continuum we may have opportunity to transmute (change the vibration of) energy patterns of experiences we had in past and future (parallel) incarnations on Earth.

As a celestial shaman, you may be re-coding detrimental patterns for people who come to you for help. Karmic patterns are held in the astral body. This "pain body" holds energetic imprints of a personality's unresolved traumas and continues to exist after the physical body dies. My retrieval and integration routine at Sweethome became applicable to my clients who were dealing with energy attachments and astral debris.

In one of my client sessions I saw an ethereal screen appear in my spirit vision. It was pulled down like a projector screen used for a slide show. My hands started moving rapidly across a grid on this morphogenic screen that had symbols something like you would see on the periodic table. Neon blue threads of light were streaming from my fingers and connected with these codes. I moved my hands intuitively as if an unlearned sign language was being communicated.

The screen allowed me to move my hands into it as if it were made of plasma or gelatin. It dawned on me that I was reaching into other timelines, dimensions, or parallel universes and pulling something from one reality to another. The codes started changing and/or swapping places within the squares on the grid. As my hands were rearranging the symbols, I sensed that I was recalibrating events and experiences of my client. Re-scripting the records of a personality's Earth trauma removes the incident from the person's experiential timeline. Or perhaps it shifts the person to an alternate reality where the experience does not exist. I had been working with this screen for about a year when I saw Halle Berry doing something similar on the show Extant. Confirmation! I see this screen on a lot of movies and TV shows.

When you are moving your hands in light language, they may start moving of their own accord, as if you are conducting an orchestra, drawing symbols in the air, gesturing for emphasis, or in an unlearned sign language. Hand movement when expressing light language may also be an indication that you are working in the Blue Morphogenic Screen.

Visualize pulling down your personal blue screen of records in front of you. Now move your hands as you speak or sing light language. You may get a sense that you are re-scripting or de-programming a childhood trauma or some type of brainwashing. There is no need to go into the story behind it. In fact, rehearsing the story could keep the old programming intact by preventing movement. This may be why talk therapy does not seem to have a long-lasting effect. It does not reach the cause or location where the energy pattern is stored. It is like deleting a file from your computer and leaving it in the recycle bin. Even if you empty the bin, the file is still on the hard drive and can be retrieved if the space has not been written over with new material. Your brain will find and restore the file as soon as an event similar to the original incident triggers you.

When integrating energy, you may feel tired, sleepy, spacey, or have soreness in your body. You may feel queasy or have headaches, etc. Take care of your physical body after you have received an energy treatment. The information I am imparting to you here may activate you in unexpected ways. You may need to put the book down and allow your body to catch up with the energy you are downloading and embodying. Rest as much as you need to. Alone time is very helpful for integration—especially if you use the RBQT-18" technique we have discussed previously in this book.

Divine Matrix Codes

If you are planning a vacation, chances are you do a little research first. Where do you want to go? What is there to do in the area? Will you stay in a hotel, resort, AirBnb, rental house, or with friends? What mode of transportation will you choose? When is the best time to go? Do you want anyone else to go with you?

Before your Spirit takes on a body, there is some pre-planning with the non-physical guides that will accompany you. Together, you come up with a "things to see and do" list so you can make the most of your incarnation. It is like an agenda or roadmap that shows possibilities for your Earth trip. This blueprint, or divine matrix codes, direct you to interface with certain people, to be at a particular location at a specific time, and to experience opportunities that will allow you to explore and grow. Think of somebody in your life that you would not have met if not for some crazy turn of events. These synchronistic meeting points are directed from your divine matrix codes.

While these plans serve us on our path as Spirit inhabiting a human body, we still have free will to make choices. Thus enters the ego (personality), which does not remember itself as part of Source's creation. Your Spirit always knows itself as Source within the body. There may be question marks on your map, or a fork in the road that you have to figure out in situ. It does not matter which way you choose; the pace of your journey is up to you. Perhaps you will decide to visit places that you did not know about before the trip began. You may meet up with old friends one evening and choose a different activity than what was on your schedule. The plan is not meant to limit you. It is a list of suggestions or specific things you might want to accomplish or experience.

Why do we have an ego? Without ego there would be no free will. Without free will, we could not make choices. All would be blissful all the time, the way it is in some dimensions or realities. This sounds kind of good right now in light of the turmoil some folks are in (and creating more of). But the rumbling we feel is the vibration of our take-off as we progress to the next dimension of our soul exploration.

Earth is meant to be an experiential amusement park complete with mirrors that distort our true image, thrilling rides, entertaining shows, spooky houses with things that jump out and scare us, long lines to wait in before we get to the next ride. It all looks fun from the other side. Our problem here is that we mistake this false reality as truth and live in fear of the fictitious things we have created.

There may be roadblocks that require you to take alternate routes, which can slow you down or provide adventures you had not counted on. Your path of exploration may lead you to make what some call "mistakes." I do wonder how anything can be a mistake if we are learning and growing from the lessons an experience provides. Each experience can inspire a greater radiance to shine within you. When you judge yourself or label an experience as bad or wrong, guilt, shame, anger, or remorse can drag you down and keep you from moving onward in your exploration. You have not lost your way when you stall—all of us will return Home eventually.

By neutralizing the trigger of life experiences, we realign with our divine matrix codes. We no longer allow things that happened in the past to control our forward movement. The influence of fearful imprinting becomes less with each seven-year cycle as we begin to live more authentically.

Seven-Year Cycles

Tragedies and traumas may cause the personality to believe that it is wounded or fragmented. Rather than trying to convince the brain that a past event is not a current reality, we can work with the image it sees in the fun house mirror. Meeting the personality at its level of comprehension is like holding a fearful child during a scary movie. Our Spirit knows the monsters are not real, but the personality needs to be guided to that discovery. We treat the personality or inner child with kindness. Spending time in the still-point field can remind us that this life is but a dream or a movie.

Imprinting in our formative years tends to play a huge role in how our personality develops and how we relate to the world and think about ourselves. While there truly are no mistakes, the first seven years of childhood development can impact us for the rest of our lives. How we will continue to respond to life is pretty much set in motion at that point. The good news is that if your codes get scrambled, they can be reset or updated. You are Spirit and you can change your course!

During the next set of seven-year cycles we start to find our individuality. However, the imprinting that occurred in the first set of seven years can cause us to deviate from expressing our true self. We have begun to accept the rules of religion, family, and society as our truth. We have learned what can be done, what cannot be done, what is acceptable, what is not, what gets us rewards, and what gets us punishment.

Shadow work is the examination of one's own internal darkness—the subconscious terrain, which lacks awareness. Part of our inner child healing or shadow work is discovering our inner truth, accepting what is, and coming back into alignment with our inner truth. Most people have no concept of shadow work. Those who do know about it may not have the courage to voluntarily participate in unearthing repressed traumas, inherited fear programs, unprocessed pain, and other disturbing and uncomfortable revelations. No matter how much we ignore, reject, and deny the shadow side of our psyche, it does not disappear until it is acknowledged. The very fear that keeps us from looking at it is the same fear that feeds it. In times of global crisis (a collective wake-up call), people are forced to look in the dark crevices of their own psyche.

As we begin our shadow work to integrate our life's experiences, we see where imprinting has been running a program in the background. I was abused by a female babysitter when I was in my formative years. In the next six sets of seven-year cycles that followed, I did not like or trust women—especially females in authority—and this caused rebellion in my teen years. As a young adult, I attracted headstrong women into my life who dominated and bossed me around, easily taking my power away just like the babysitter did. I could be friends with men, but not with women.

Source and your team of helpers always look for ways to help you resolve and integrate life's experiences. They are ready to meet you right where you are. The betrayals by overbearing women in my early adult years triggered the original incident that misaligned my divine matrix codes, thereby offering me an opportunity to address the subconscious loss of power I experienced as a child, clear the resulting patterns, and move forward. I did not recognize this until I was in my fifties; however, since then I find it easy to have friendships with women and to open my heart to them.

There are a lot of processes that you may use to reset the codes of your original blueprint when they have gotten hacked. During one of my celestial shaman workshops, we worked with the blue morphogenic screen to reset or realign with our original codes as well as bring in more codes to support our current and future paths. Think of these new codes as an upgrade to your personal operating system— technology from the stars. Each participant in the workshop generated a field with their technicians and team members to work with us on clearing imprints in their emotional and physical components. While lying on the floor, each person used light language to initiate vector movement that would locate anomalies from each of the seven-year cycles. The energy rose as we called forth this work into our first-year cycle (birth to age seven). When the energy waned, we knew that cycle was complete. We paused for a moment of integration and then began resetting the codes that went askew during the second seven-year cycle (ages eight to fourteen).

Once we got past the ninth seven-year cycle, where the oldest person in our group was currently at age-wise, we felt the need to keep going. I sensed that our technicians were installing maintenance devices to assure future realigning of patterns that had been skewed in the previous cycles.

There are many ways to do shadow work. My life shifted dramatically and quickly after I read a book written by Michael Brown titled The Presence Process. The ten-week process took a lot of dedication, but I became more determined than ever to follow my heart and find the joy that was missing in my life. "I am here now in this!" is a mantra from Brown's book that I still use when I find myself anxious, frustrated, or speaking negatively about myself or a situation.

Conscious breathing is a positive way to interact with an energetic imprint so it can be released and integrated. A circular breath has no pause at the top of the inhale or at the bottom of the exhale. It is best done through the nose for at least five minutes or until you start to sense an indication that you have connected with Spirit. I practiced a circular type of breathing with a women's group in 2013-2014 and found it very cathartic. We released all kinds of childhood dysfunction. I encourage you to consciously breathe in this manner and experience the expansion it brings. The new alignment brings outward results. You may notice a difference in how you think and behave afterward, and how people relate to you. With a new perspective you can make better decisions. Addictions may fall away. Synchronistic meetings occur. In this restorative process, creativity begins to flourish, and joy flows, and new perspectives come.

Sitting in silent still-point is a wonderful way to restore your personal divine matrix codes. When you are in the present moment feeling what you feel without assigning judgement, ask Spirit to move through you to help integrate life's experiences and bring freedom. When we get into a place where we are really focused on our feelings and not our story, all kinds of information pops in. Our felt sensations start to arise, tears come to the surface as we move past anger, blame, and disappointment. When the mind is quiet you will sense Spirit calling you into alignment. Do you feel something in your body right now? Tune in.

By integrating our life experiences, we restore and reconnect with our divine matrix codes. As we free ourselves of imprints that focus outward and on performance, we affect the human race in a positive way. Thus we are able to assist in shifting the collective paradigm. We begin to live authentically and teach others how to lessen the effects of imprinting in each generation.

CHAPTER 7 ~ Following Your Inner Guidance

"Intuition literally means learning from within. Most of us were not taught how to use this sense, but all of us know well this 'gut' feeling. Learn to trust your inner feeling and it will become stronger. Avoid going against your better judgment or getting talked into things that just do not feel right."

~ Doe Anatamata

I was playing Minecraft with my grandson, who was nine years old at the time. I do not know how to play Minecraft. He is an expert. As I held the controller, he sat next to me, watching anxiously, and commenting on my every move. I was discovering something new at every turn and exploring how to build very pixelated square thingies. It was fun. I could see myself spending/wasting hours trying to learn this game.

To my grandson, it appeared that I was not getting anywhere or making any progress. His instructions were helpful, for sure. "Turn here. Grab that. Go to your house. Put it there." But I could tell he was becoming frustrated with me not knowing what to do. Finally, he could stand it no longer. My incompetency with the game was just too much. He grabbed the controller from my hands and started playing my game for me! I laughed as I realized the spiritual application in what had just happened.

Many spiritual teachers do not teach people how to find their own inner guidance. They do not allow their students to have their own methods and opinions that come from discoveries they make along the way. They tell them what to believe. Some expect their students to be at the same expert playing level as the teacher. And, when they do not measure up, some "gurus" take control of the student. Well-meaning advice turns into manipulation.

In my church days, I was force-fed dogma. From the pulpit, I was told what I could wear, where I could go, what music I could listen to, and how to live my life. Back then, I did not realize that the fundamentalist doctrine was robbing me of my ability to think for myself. Asking questions was frowned upon. When I disagreed with a decision of the leadership, I was abruptly dismissed from my position as the church pianist and teacher in that church's Christian School.

I had been a rebel in my teen years, but I started to surrender my will to others during young adulthood. I was married for the first time at age seventeen. I was taught that wives should submit to their husbands in all things. Women were not to speak in church. Children who did not obey were to be punished. Because of my overzealousness to please the pastor (and therefore, God) my son's self-esteem was ruined by my harsh parenting method. I prayed, worshipped Jesus and Jehovah, sang hymns, read my Bible, and played piano for hours each day rather than playing or having fun with my son. I was taught that "fun" was spelled "s-i-n." Yes, that was actually said multiple times during sermons at one church I attended.

By the time my daughter was born, I had begun to see the error of my ways. I modified my parenting style and became more lenient and compassionate. But it was hard to let go of the teachings that I believed kept me in right standing with God. Even though this controlling Judaic deity could not be pleased, I was still afraid of his wrath. I had too much fear to leave organized religion cold turkey. Our family changed churches several times, finding a little more freedom with each move, but still clinging to the doctrine that we were all sinners in need of punishment. When I finally left organized religion in my early forties, I was bitter and angry, and my rebellion had returned. My inner fire and self-worth were at an all-time low. My beliefs had let me down, and I began seeking a better way to have a relationship with the divine. Simultaneously, I was beginning to doubt God even existed.

How can anyone find their own truth when they are being forced to believe or accept the ideas, methods, and beliefs of another person? Have you ever felt that you were expected to believe the same way as someone else in order to be accepted by them?

It is common for spiritual teachers to read books, attend lectures, and search the internet for information to guide them on their spiritual path. When the information we get from others replaces (rather than confirms) our inner guidance, we give away our power. Do you trust your inner knowing, or are you still expecting someone else to confirm or deny your worth or the validity of your experience? If you look for validation outside yourself, you may be disappointed.

Well-meaning teachers in the spiritual community try to control others by imposing their beliefs on members of the group. CeCe, a client of mine, activated her light language in one of my monthly online classes. As she sang and danced around her house, practicing this new gift, she was uplifted and excited about the positive changes she was seeing. Since then, she has overcome many health problems using light language, gratitude, and self-love. Her light language has also blessed me many times.

CeCe was also working with a spiritual mentor who was helping her heal a health issue that had recently come up. CeCe played an audio for her mentor of some light language she and I had recorded. The mentor said she could only listen to a couple of minutes of it because it had an "evil entity attachment." CeCe's confidence and joy immediately deflated and turned into confusion and fear. "How can a language which felt so positive to me be evil?" CeCe asked. "Why would an evil entity speak through me? That makes no sense!"

Inwardly, CeCe did not believe what the mentor said, but her words keep coming back and stirring up more doubt and fear. Soon, she noticed that something had changed in the way her light language sounded although she believed she could easily return to the former version. CeCe trusted her mentor because she had helped her heal physically. Therefore, she allowed herself to believe her mentor's cruel judgment of her light language.

After a few days, CeCe contacted me feeling completely perplexed and downhearted. I reminded her that light language has the ability to stir up things that need to be resolved in all of us. It would naturally stir up some unresolved energy that her mentor/healer needed to deal with. When people do not understand something new, they may feel as though they are losing control of something within themselves. When something feels unfamiliar or pushes them to the edge of their comfort zone, many people will try to stop the upsetting activity (in this case, light language) in order to avoid feeling what they are feeling. Labeling something as "evil" is a quick way to make someone stop what they are doing and doubt the legitimacy of their gift/guidance. The need to control or change someone else or their experience can be destructive. This is a perfect example of why it is so important to trust what you feel rather than what someone else says.

Once we exchanged a couple of emails, CeCe started feeling like her bubbly self and promised herself that she would not be silenced again. Last I heard from her she was going to create something beautiful! Bravo, CeCe!

Please, never allow fear or what someone else says to rob you of your joy. Know the difference between your personal truth and what has been projected upon you by others. Your happiness is a powerful vibration that helps hold a higher frequency while humanity is shifting. Fear never serves your well-being.

Here is another example of minding someone else's business and interfering with someone's personal path of progress. During a recent gathering, some women began giving unsolicited advice to a young man about controlling his sexual expression. Being energy sensitive, I could tell he felt attacked and shamed by them. Yet, he did not oppose or contradict them. He wanted to do what was "right" and please those he considered his teachers. I guess this triggered me because of how my upbringing took away my power. I was not allowed to choose how I wanted to express my sexuality. Sex could only be had within the fear-based rules set forth by the church or Bible. Urging our youth to not have sex until married seems like a good way to help them avoid sexually transmitted diseases and unwanted pregnancy; however, it is actually a form of control. I believe it is better to teach kids how to explore responsibly and manage their sexual impulses from a higher perspective.

"There is a voice inside you that whispers all day long. 'I feel this is right for me. I know that this is wrong.' No teacher, preacher, parent, friend, or wise man can decide what's right for you—just listen to the voice that speaks inside."

~ Shel Silverstein

Being thrown into the pool of life to either sink or swim has been the typical method of learning for me. Like my mom, I graduated from the School of Hard Knocks and Experiences. I have never had a spiritual guru. In fact, I am reluctant to listen to channeled messages or watch videos that teach others how to better their lives, which is ironic considering my mission is to assist those who have encountered a loss of power through their life experiences. I have never had anyone teach me how to do a job at any occupation I have undertaken. Things were sometimes left in a mess by my predecessors, which required me to straighten out the budget, reorganize operational procedures, improve staff relationships, and take the blame for the poor management created by the one who held the position before me. At one job, I was asked to create my own job description! Such is the norm for way-showers and path-setters.

I have been a leader for as long as I can remember. Even as an adolescent I noticed that there was a big difference in what the Bible said about relationships and what I saw in my home. My rebellion and peacekeeping attempts were mostly ignored, or they got me into trouble. Slowly, I found myself conforming to the wishes of the church and expectations of the adults in my life. My personal freedom was eroding, and I was learning to ignore the inner voice of my intuition. I was miserable as a teenager. Depression, that lasted well into my adulthood, set in.

Churches, politicians, and educational systems reiterate information and reinforce beliefs that are already commonly accepted. These systems allow very little hands-on exploration of our inner truth or a better way to live. Many political leaders do not direct society toward positive change. They made rules to help them accomplish their objectives with little regard to the well-being of the population. Everywhere we look, someone else has the remote control to our belief system and is calling the shots. We cannot legislate morality. Our values must come from our higher, intuitive guidance. Unfortunately, we have been taught not to trust that guidance.

When we take a channeled message and try to make it fit our belief system, or make our beliefs fit someone else's ideals, we rob ourselves of the joy of discovering our inner truth. As mentioned, I purposefully avoid channeled teachings and predictions. If I read something on the internet or read a book about a spiritual topic, it is because it finds me through synchronicity. I can tell if the material resonates with me by how it feels and whether or not it confirms what I have already been pondering in my heart. My clients find me in much the same way.

> "Stay true to yourself. Do not worry about what people think of you or about the way they try to make you feel. If people want to see you as a good person, they will. If they want to see you as a bad person, absolutely nothing you do will stop them.

Ironically, the more you try to show them your good intentions, the more reason you give them to knock you down if they are committed to misunderstanding you. Keep your head up high and be confident in what you do. Be confident in your intentions and keep your eyes ahead instead of wasting your time on those who want to drag you back. Because you cannot change people's views, you have to believe that true change for yourself comes from within you, not from anyone else."

~ Najwa Zebian

I now see how the controlling people in my life were set up to upset me so I would find my voice and stand up for my own truth. Due to being so controlled by religion, I now tend to balk at anything that reeks of formality, tradition, or doctrine. Living authentically in one's personal power is an important part of being a celestial shaman. It is also a process that requires unification of the personality so it aligns with higher directives.

It is very rewarding to take back control of your life. Yes, it may upset a few people along the way, mainly the ones who benefit most by your over-accommodating efforts. Be prepared to not allow their reactions to pull you off course. Using the blue triangle vector method, you will be able to stand in your personal truth, make course corrections, and follow your inner guidance—even when others are trying to grab the controller out of your hands.

Speaking Up for Yourself

Why is it so hard to speak up in a situation that is causing us angst? Do we really value the thoughts, opinions, and agendas of others, or is it that we have such little respect and trust for ourselves? I think both may be true. We have been taught to obey without question and stay quiet in order to be accepted by our peers and those in authority. We have not been taught to honor our inner knowing.

When something causes you to feel uncomfortable it is because the situation is out of alignment with your truth. The time to say something is when you first begin to feel annoyed—as soon as your body begins to feel tense and before you get angry. When we stay in a situation or relationship past the point of upset, we have stayed too long.

I went to a creative writing class at a community center that did not start on time. In fact, the class did not start at all, even though there were six people sitting around the table where I had assumed we would be writing from a prompt given by the teacher or reading what others had written as a homework assignment. After half an hour, people were still coming in and some were checking email on their phones to see who had sent word that they were not coming. I assumed we were waiting others to arrive.

This appeared to be a gossip session for the above-fifty crowd. It was obvious that everyone there knew one another and everything about their families, including their pets, past and present. That is how I finally discovered that the teacher was the one sitting at the end of the table.

An hour later, I was so frustrated I wanted to scream. I had an internal battle going on in my head. I wanted to excuse myself and leave, but I could not get a word in edgewise. I could have just walked out but I did not want to seem rude. Always looking for a higher purpose, I thought that perhaps there was something I could learn in this situation or some connection I would make as a result of being there.

Being the newcomer, I awaited my turn to introduce myself to the group. So far, each person had taken fifteen to twenty minutes to say something about themselves that they would not mind having repeated publicly. When my turn came, I had only spoken about three sentences (including that I needed to leave at 11:30, which was in fifteen minutes) when someone interrupted me to add a ten-minute detail they had forgotten to include when it was their turn. My turn never came around again and I was feeling agitated. Not because I felt I had anything important that anyone needed to know about me, but because I was not getting what I expected from this "class."

One thing I cannot stand is the old "bait and switch" routine in which someone promises one thing and then delivers something different that is not up to par. To me, that kind of deception is the same as lying. I suppose that is why I was feeling so frustrated that day. My higher guidance wanted me to speak up, set a boundary, and not suffer through this any longer. The observer part of me was amused at what was transpiring. How silly this was! How patient I must be! It was like I was magnetized to the chair and my lips were superglued shut.

A second and similar opportunity came less than a month later when I attended my first writer's Meetup group. Four people sat around the table. We made introductions and swapped business cards. We shared the names of book cover artists, printing vendors, and upcoming events in the writing and publishing industry. That was done in about twenty minutes and the conversation waned. None of us brought any writing to share. The man next to me, who had a full beard on his earlobes as well as his face, smelled like he forgot to clean up during his last trip to the bathroom. I remembered the misery I had endured at the community center and decided I would not do that again. I wanted to go home. The mental battle started again, but this time I would not worry about what others thought or said about me. As soon as I saw a break, I excused myself and left. I was proud of myself for taking action quickly.

Feelings & Empathic Gifts

We have been shamed into not trusting our intuition. We have been taught that we need to look to someone or somewhere outside of ourselves for validation. Highly empathic people have been told that they are too sensitive. Because we experience life in a sensory manner, we have been told that we live in an imaginary world that does not exist. Everything we can imagine can exist. There are as many realities, truths, and points of view as there are people to experience them. Like the book series, Choose Your Own Adventure, Spirit has infinite free will and can choose its own reality. We can live by a truth that is uniquely ours rather than adopting and retrofitting someone else's truth to override our own. Thus, each of us can and have created our own experience, individually and collectively. This may seem hard to accept when we see so much chaos around us. "I would not create that," you might say. Modifying your truth to match someone else's or to fit into a corrupt social system keeps undesirable behaviors and frequencies intact by default. When you are concerned with managing your own 18 inches, you will begin to see how you can be in the world and not of it. You will experience peace that surpasses your understanding.

Thought forms are like seeds that have the opportunity to grow once they are planted, consciously or unconsciously, in the soil of our mind. Much like a virus, we can implant infections in each other through our beliefs, ideas, and sharing of information. It can be challenging to keep an open heart during a collective flow of change. In troublesome times (and in daily life), your experience will be whatever you draw to yourself as truth—either yours or someone else's.

"The universe only understands the frequency in which you are vibrating. If you are vibrating in the frequency of fear, guilt, or shame, you are going to attract things of a similar vibration. If you are vibrating in the frequency of love, joy, and abundance, you are going to attract things that support that frequency. It is kind of like tuning into a radio station. You have to be tuning in to the music you want to listen to just like you have to be tuned into the energy you want to manifest into your life. Change your mindset; it will change your life."

~ Unknown

Many of you reading this have been practicing unification of your personality and have been focusing on ascension for a while. You are accustomed to balancing what you read/hear on the news and staying grounded so as not to be swept away by fear. You have been practicing inner peace, watching your thoughts, and managing your emotions. You have stayed connected to Source and your body through meditation, yoga, and other spiritual practices. As you anchor divine love into this realm, you are holding space for resolving humanity's challenges. Thank you for holding a joyful vibration of gratitude while facing the unknown.

Times of crisis bring a "pattern interrupt" to our collective, habitual ways of operating on autopilot which are focused on excessive materialism, distraction, and destructive productivity. As I type this, people are currently staying at home due to the coronavirus, which is offering some powerful focus. It is like someone pushed the pause button on the rat race! We are rapidly becoming grateful for things we once took for granted. We are economizing and reducing our carbon footprint as a result. Those who are willing to detach from panic are able to sense a deeper truth emerging from the rubble. There is an incredible portal open now that will move us into a new collective reality. Are you ready to take a quantum leap and rebirth as the best, most authentic version of yourself?

When humanity is suffering, sensitive empaths may feel it. These times urge us to dream of a better future. I certainly feel the ripples in the collective consciousness and have plenty of opportunities to allow fear to set in. Even though uncomfortable feelings tend to arise, I have a sense of inner peace. I appreciate those who are on the frontlines caring for the sick and dying and those trying to make sure we have food available. While I care about what others are experiencing, it does not do them or me any good to be fearful. Bringing fear into any situation is a mental or linear practice of the ego. The world has had enough of living from a place of fear. Every day I feel grateful to be healthy and whole. I am confident about what the future holds because I see this pandemic as a tool for self-adjustment and for creating a new, uplifted global paradigm. We are consciously co-creating the planet we have always wanted. Everything not aligned with love—businesses, systems, practices, beliefs, traditions, fears—will be dismantled or rearranged. Through love all things are possible, including individual and planetary healing. This pandemic could end up being the most profound and valuable thing that has ever happened in our lifetime.

The body is a great way to get messages from your guidance. We receive instructions through all sensory mechanisms in the body as well as through our intuition, which has an unexplainable ability to know what it knows on a deeper level. This feeling-sensing nature holds clues and information about what is going on in our subconscious and can show us where Spirit wants to work through us.

Celestial shamans may sense energy as discomfort in the body or as an emotion that comes on suddenly and without provocation. Some have an ability to smell, hear, or taste energy. They may get images or see visions. Those who work with clients have many ways to discern where their celestial team is working. We still have to interpret these sensory "clues" in order to understand them. For example, I have found it common for people to feel a lump or pressure in their throat when their light language is birthing. I may feel it in my throat when a client is opening to this vocal expression. The discomfort could be an indication that the client needs to be more direct in expressing their feelings and desires. If I sense this to be the case, I will mention it to them. They still have to interpret the message or feeling and how this applies to them.

Sensory input you receive right before or while working with a client will dissipate as things shift in their field. I used to go through a "clearing" protocol after working with clients. I smudged with sage so often that we had to change the HVAC filters every month! Everything is done with intention now. As the separation mentality is less active, you naturally live from your inner sanctuary in a way that is true to your calling. From this place of stillness, you gain insight. If there is some action to take, it will be revealed. Synchronicities will cause your path to unfold and things fall into place. Everything you need will be provided.

When using light language, I connect with higher realms of pure love; therefore, I do not worry about being protected from something out there trying to "get me." The practice of maintaining the energy in my personal energy cylinder surrounding my body naturally creates a strong field of light around me. I am so intimately aware of how my own energy feels, I can quickly note when something is pushing in toward me.

The more you maintain your personal vortex of 18 inches, the less you need to be concerned with being attacked or doing harm to another. You know what you have to do to keep yourself physically safe. It may be as simple as not allowing yourself to be in a place (or relationship) where the vibration is consistently low or dangerous. It could mean you do not let your body get fatigued, which can make you vulnerable.

If you do not realize that your body can be used as a guidance tool, you may completely miss its messages and think you are sick or that something is wrong. Being in your 18-inch personal still-point naturally drowns out contrary thoughts or voices. There are several ways to get to the unified still-point of your Spirit, body, and personality. Some people find it helpful to stare into water or a flame. Meditation works well for others. The steady rhythm of a drum, speaking and singing light language, or a nature walk gets me in the zone. Our experience in human form is a personal one. My clients are responding beautifully to the RBQT-18" practice that helps them know what their own energy feels like. I taught the Reset Breath©, Quiet Touch, and how to feel the 18-inch personal field to one client who had been meditating for an hour a day. She reached a deep still-point within sixty seconds.

Here is an example of a simple practice to help you calm your body and get into the zero-point field.

1. Place your left palm on your chest and discover where you feel the strongest energy.
2. Place your right hand on your abdomen above the pubic bone.
3. Complete a Reset Breath© and become aware of your personal space.
4. Take a deep breath and move your focus to various places within your body.
5. Deeply feel your personal energy field as it interfaces with your body. Move your hands around in that space which belongs to you.
6. Breathe in and begin a long nasal tone of "ohm," or speak/tone light language. Allow the sound to vibrate inside your head and nasal cavity.
7. Pause the tone and notice what has shifted. Does the magnetic field around your body feel more alive and tangible? Have your thoughts become quieter?
8. Now, take a Reset Breath© and tone again.
9. Repeat this awareness exercise several times, going deeper into a calm, relaxed space each time. Then, sit in the stillness of your inner sanctuary. Recognize the frequency of your own energy. Feel vibrations in your body and energy field. You may notice that external sounds have become part of your vibration rather than a distraction.

How does it feel to be in your own energy, the presence of your higher self? Common responses include "expanded, free of doubt, confident or sure of myself, peaceful, whole,

Home, knowing who I really am, grateful, blessed, quiet inside my mind, in sync, in the flow, etc."

While in the stillness, rekindle a relationship with your inner child. Speak kindly to yourself—even if you feel frustrated about some decision you made or something that upset you. Be your own best friend. Let the waves of unconditional love flow over you and through you. Feel, know, sense, and receive!

Society has typically shunned highly sensitive people who easily express their emotions. Empaths have been misunderstood and criticized for their sensitivity. Because of this conditioning, we tend to put labels on our feelings. Emotions are part of personality and how we express ourselves. There is no need to judge them as good or bad. The response to emotions is to simply feel them—even the hard ones. If we only allow ourselves to express "good" feelings, we limit our ability to process energy and intimately know ourselves. Resistance to feel may push away an energy pattern that could be resolved with our loving attention. If we label some emotions as bad and some as good we cannot live in the moment, which requires us to be present with whatever experience we are encountering.

Feeling angry about something can be a healthy first step toward resolution. It does not define your future or your identity. Your feelings do not have to dictate your actions. If you are focused on loving and accepting yourself, you will learn to understand and love yourself in a new way that is not based upon performance. Self-love will begin to shift how you interact with life and others. Self-talk is telling. If you want to monitor the integration progress of your personality, notice your inner dialogue. The very process is bringing you into greater alignment with a universe that always supports you.

It can feel satisfying to honor feelings of depression somedays. Crying is a good thing. It can bring release. If you want to stay in your pain, you get to do that. If you want to laugh and play, you can do that too, on this day or another. You get to feel whatever you feel. Know that you are safe feeling and expressing an emotion. My pillow has muffled many soul screams!

There are a lot of food choices offered an all-you-can-eat buffet. You do not have to put every type of food on your plate. You can select what you want and leave the rest. You may go back for seconds, or at a later date, and make totally different choices. You are not locked into making the same selection as last time. If someone, who is minding your business instead of their own, puts undesired food on your plate, you do not have to eat it! There is nothing wrong with the food; you simply do not want it. You may have to set boundaries and ask people not to mess with your plate. The same is true with energy. We have choices about what we allow ourselves to take on and digest. We can accept and feel emotions and use them to create a different experience in life.

Many people fear the integration process of the personality. I know of people who have found their identity in being an overwhelmed empath. They are reluctant to let go of the habit of taking on the energy around them even though they claim to be miserable. A deep introspection of your secrets, shadow side, desires, and longings can be transforming. It can also be scary if you do not know how to deal with your feelings or fear being taken down by them. Who knows what buggers might be lurking in the dark? There is nothing wrong with you just because a wayward thought from the collective field pings you.

When we are confident in our worthiness to be loved, we will not be so affected by the experiences that others are creating for themselves. We will not feel inclined to fix things that are not ours to fix. We will know the truth of who we are, and that truth will set us free.

Feeling Like You Have No Emotions

People are activating their sensory abilities to feel energy more than they ever have before. So why do we sometimes feel robotic or seem to have no feelings at all? Empaths are accustomed to feeling everything, all the time. Some highly sensitive people have expressed concern that they are being taken over by a negative entity when they get off the emotional rollercoaster. Perhaps they are unfamiliar with how it feels to not be controlled by emotions.

If you are not having emotions, it is natural to wonder if you are shutting down your feelings. Have you considered that feeling somewhat robotic might mean that you are in a neutral or surrendered position? There is a tendency to think something is wrong when a neutral state arrives.

To me, feeling non-emotional is natural for those who are learning to manage energy. Choosing not to feel the pain of others is not a lack of compassion. It is a realization that our feeling bad does not help anyone else feel better. When we stop allowing our emotional energy to be siphoned, we are likely to feel lighter or feel nothing at all.

While I was processing my divorce, there were days when I felt very little emotion. My human side tried to convince me that there was something wrong because I did not feel grief, loss, or sadness. Not only was I leaving a man I had loved for many years, I was leaving Sweethome and the healing woods. Part of the ministry I had built there would have to end or shift in order to accommodate my new life. Trust, faith, surrender, and being fully present became more important than ever!

A neutral position does not mean that we do not have emotion. We are never outside of emotion. There is always vibration or movement in the field. Rather, we have no need to interface with emotional energy. What is in someone else's field may not be any of our business. We do not have to engage it—unless we want to. We do not have to bring it in. We do not have to define it. We might observe that the field is bumpy or erratic at times, but that is an observation, not an experience. Emotion can vibrate in your field and not disturb your inner calm. It can be felt without taking over.

As part of my training in emotional energy management, my guidance led me to watch several seasons of Grey's Anatomy. This very touching drama series gave me plenty of practice in controlling how I respond to emotional and physical pain that others are experiencing. Our brains do not know the difference between what our eyes see on a TV show and what is happening right in front of us. Past events and projected future scenarios can seem just as real as if they were happening present tense if we allow our emotions to follow that rabbit trail. We have the power to control what we focus our attention on.

But shouldn't we feel blissful? We can if we learn to respond maturely to emotional energy. Repressing our feelings is not the same as acknowledging and processing feelings without succumbing to the emotional energy they contain. Managing energy means we work with the energy. We do not ignore it.

We do not try to banish it. Once we recognize an unpleasant emotion and are done experiencing it, we change its energetic pattern or let it go. We have resolved the energy pattern when we are no longer triggered when we think of the situation.

I appreciate the diversity that my Earth experience provides. Feelings and emotions are energy that can be moved and molded, sensed or ignored. I can ride the adventurous wave of whatever arises, or intentionally call up any feeling I want to experience.

We are learning to better manage energy. We realize that nothing has power or control over us unless we give it permission. Feelings and thoughts represent options. The outcome, or our emotional condition, is a result of how we respond to these thoughts and feelings. Thoughts and feelings that pop in uninvited offer us an opportunity to shift our perspective and put us in touch with our true self.

CHAPTER 8 ~ Soul Purpose vs. Your Mission

Many people equate soul purpose with goal-based achievements. Clients often ask me, "What is my soul purpose?" and "How do I manifest my mission?"

Your soul purpose is your private experience and inner journey toward Home. This personal unification process includes being loving and kind to yourself and being fully present as consistently as you can. Your worth and your soul purpose have nothing to do with your accomplishments.

Mission is your ministry or work. It is how you "do unto others." Your service-based mission is expressed when you take time to listen to someone who needs companionship. It can be the act of doubling a blessing by "paying it forward." It could be helping a turtle get safely across the road or helping someone tie his shoes. When you act out of kindness, compassion, and love, you are accomplishing your mission.

Ego would have you think you should be doing more. Maybe you think you should be doing spiritual stuff instead of working in a corporate setting. Your mission can unfold as an expression of love regardless of who your employer is.

The line between the sacred and the secular is imaginary. It is a product of the belief in separation—us and them. Your work is an occupation that earns money. Your mission may also provide income for you. Relationships provide lessons for personal development and offers opportunities to share your journey, your love, and wisdom with others. As you interface with the world in whatever job you choose, there are opportunities for your mission to unfold.

Working without a sense of stress or fear is pure joy—especially if your work involves doing something you love and feel drawn to. Like anything else in life, an attitude of gratitude boosts our level of happiness. The speed at which we evolve is determined by how often we express gratitude. The happier we are, the more aligned with Spirit we become. By being grateful and living consciously in each situation, your job can be your mission.

If your job/work is not bringing joy, notice your attitude towards life in general.

- Do you accept your personality and its perceived flaws without judgment?
- Are you showing kindness to yourself in everyday situations?
- Are you spending time in stillness where divine direction naturally drops in?
- How are you managing your personal 18 inches?
- Are you filling your life with distractions?
- Are you developing an intimate relationship with yourself as Source?
- Do you view other people as toxic and blame them for your unhappiness?
- Is your vibration uplifting to your work environment and coworkers?

If you find it difficult to manifest your mission, you may be trying too hard to make things happen. Being grateful for where you are right now is vitally important to creating movement and flowing into something better. You will either shift your attitude to better manage being around negativity, or you will shift out of the unpleasant job altogether and find a new place to offer your skills and services.

Music was very important to me in my younger years. Since I spent so much of my time in church, I created music and involved myself with people there who loved to sing and make music. It is only natural that my job (making a living) and my soul mission (inner journey) would incorporate music. My first job was in a music store where I taught piano lessons and rang sales at the register. I also taught piano at home for twenty-five years, starting at age sixteen.

As a child, I sang alto next to Zelda Bagley in our Southern Baptist church choir. My mom, who has always been supportive of me, got me an electric chord organ for Christmas when I was nine years old. I found it delightful to match the left-hand push-button chords with a simple melody in my right hand. Noticing this, Mom decided to get me a real piano and let me take lessons. She would rush home from work, grab me and my brother from our grandmother's house, and fight the afternoon traffic to a music store across town where I learned sight reading, theory, and classical music. I had good teachers and learned something vital from each of them. But none of them could help me develop my natural talent for playing by ear. So, we switched my lessons to Mrs. Marshall, a piano teacher who conveniently lived across the street. I learned what I could from her and made great progress, but after a year or so, my natural ability was crying out for specific instruction on improvisation.

As the other kids were running around playing while the grownups talked before and after church service, I watched our pianists, Mrs. Glover and Mozell Brewer, practice songs with soloists and duets who were scheduled to present songs in the service next week. When a quartet or choir would visit our church, I would ask the pianists to show me what they did on a particular song.

By the time I was thirteen or fourteen, I was playing for our youth choir and my parents' quartet, as well as for funerals and weddings. I learned to use foot pedals, slide stops, and push buttons on the old Hammond organ. When our church organist left, I took her position and played for the choir and congregational singing. I was the natural choice for church pianist when Mrs. Brewer left. I was sixteen.

Mom drove me long distances to learn improvisation from Joyce Demos, Richard McGaha, and Cindy, whose last name I cannot remember. I call her the "boom-chop-chop teacher" because she taught me an important three-quarter time left-hand rhythm that revolutionized my playing. I practiced for hours at home each week. As I put all the learning together, my own playing style emerged with bits and pieces from each teacher intermingled. I was composing sonatas, imitating the style of Floyd Cramer, and was adept at Southern Gospel techniques. After marrying my first husband at age seventeen, he and I moved to another church where I took a paid position as the church/choir pianist and began embellishing hymn arrangements for preludes, processionals, and offertories.

When I began to add light language to my playing in the mid-1990s, my style morphed into a very intuitive energetic expression from my soul. Music continues to be part of my work and my soul purpose. Once I saw what was unfolding I put forth the effort to incorporate all my interests into my mission/ministry, which came about naturally.

I love to teach and share what I learn. I have used my teaching talent as a music teacher, a preschool teacher, author, mother, and grandmother. I am an excellent organizer who can solve problems. I am good with inspiring and leading people to discover their own strengths. These skills came in handy when I was asked to take the position as the director of the preschool where I was enjoying teaching a class of three-year olds. Math has never been my strong suit, but as director I was responsible for doing payroll, keeping financial records, accounting, and project an annual budget. It was also my first experience with computers, which back in the late 1980s ran on DOS.

When I lived in Muncie, Indiana, I worked at a Christian bookstore as the curriculum administrator. This opened opportunities for me to work with nearly every church in town. Soon, I was participating in prayer meetings and filling in as pianist for worship services in several denominations throughout the city. I led a women's prayer group in my home.

These skills were expanded upon later when I started working as the mayor's assistant in a small town near Nashville. I found daily opportunities to turn my coworkers' gossip sessions into enlightening conversations that led to my facilitating prayer meetings and Bible studies. I brought the community together through planning town events. My writing was published as press releases in the local paper. I assisted the planning commission by taking notes at their meetings. I worked with the drug task force and a domestic violence team. I started the town's first chamber of commerce.

When I divorced in 2000, I received no alimony or financial assistance and had to make enough money to support myself. I started taking temp jobs with Randstad Staffing Agency and learned much about the business world and Microsoft Suite, which came in handy when I landed a permanent full-time job. I was there for five years and enjoyed interacting with people—many who were disgruntled and unhappy. Of course, there were things about the corporate system that I did not like, but I have always been able to put things in perspective and find my Pollyanna joy within.

Writing was my favorite subject in high school. I wrote short stories when my children were young. The first book I published was a humorous account of their teen years as I transitioned through a divorce from their father. This natural talent that I enjoyed led me to starting my business, Writers in the Sky, which provided ghostwriting and editing services to hundreds of clients. Within a year, I had more projects than I could do. I subcontracted writers and editors to take the more technical projects while I continued to work with people who needed help with writing and editing on spiritual topics. I knew it was time to let go of that "occupation" when I realized I was doing as much coaching as I was writing and editing. I loved coaching and this provided a natural segue to using light language and music to help people shift when words failed to do the job.

At some point in my journey I was led to be part of Toastmasters. I really did not know why I was feeling a need to learn public speaking until I started Writers in the Sky Podcast, which shared information about writing, editing, and book marketing. Since many of the authors I interviewed were talking about spiritual topics, that podcast morphed into We Are One in Spirit Podcast.

I am saying all this to help you see that the point of life is daily living. Finding your mission does not have to be any more complicated than walking through doors that open synchronically for you. It seemed natural to learn while I was doing my best at whatever challenge was presented. Knowledge and understanding came as I followed my heart and let life unfold. I was not concerned about making a huge impact on the world or making a lot of money. My goal was and is to be successful in my own eyes, to surrender to divine will, and be happy wherever I am.

Life is about enjoying the journey and being present in as many moments as you can. Regardless of whether you accomplish some great act or deed, you are beautiful in your own way. What you do each and every day is enough to change the part of the world that you influence. Having goals is a good thing, but do not let them be a distraction or an obsession. That is not to say that you sit around and do nothing. It means that whatever action you take is Spirit-directed and inspired by your higher consciousness.

Many times, I have wondered, What if I had chosen a different path? Would I now be happier? I realize that every decision I make has a future outcome. Worrying about the past or the future is only helpful if you like being stuck. Dragging emotional baggage and past regret around with you is counterproductive to living fully in the moment. When faced with a decision in life, try not to fret over it too much. By following your guidance in any given moment, you will end up exactly where you need to be. You will gain resources, feel satisfied, and have opportunity to help others and share your love.

If what you have right now is good, be thankful for it. Do not overlook the riches right in front of your eyes. When you live in a state of gratitude, material things do not mean much. You appreciate them, but you do not identify with them to the point of not being able to live without them.

If the life you have created so far is not what you want to continue to experience, you can either change it or accept it as it is. Life may be uncomfortable at times. Things will not always go as you hope. You may feel grief or disappointment. Abiding in your inner sanctuary with your Spirit, you can find strength to persevere through your current hardship or find the courage to move on. There may be times when the personality enjoys hardship. Personally, I have found little meaning in suffering. Staying too long in sadness or negative emotions seems to prolong and promote more of the same. But that is your choice. There is no wrong or right way to live.

Outside influences try to distract us from the spiritual realm within. If someone disagrees with how you live your life or criticize the choices you make, do not change just to please them. They may choose to live their life how they want, but that does not mean you should hold back your joy or align with what they say is best. If you want to live a certain way, do it without apology. You do not need to play small to help someone else feel secure. Repressing your truth or denying your needs so others feel comfortable can distort your guidance.

Outside information that confirms what your inner guidance has been revealing can be helpful. When you get conflicting feedback from another person it is just that—a feedback or reflection of what they believe. Your outer world reflects your inner world. If there is turmoil inside, you may experience it outwardly. And you may even blame others for the discord. Chaos around you reflects what is in the collective field. You get to choose whether or not to participate. If you create drama, you will continue to reflect a reality that makes your life difficult. The best thing you can do in those moments is to sit with the experience, feel it in your body, and ask Spirit for direction. The confirmation may come randomly through another person or situation. It could come through triggers, which are messengers reminding you to deal with repressed emotions.

The opposite is true as well. When you live from the inside out, when you are truly in touch and paying attention to feelings and sensations in your body, you become keenly aware of your divine connection. Discernment becomes second nature.

I face many of the same challenges and discomforts as you. It might seem as though I have life figured out, but I promise you I have had my share of trouble and sorrow. I try to take things one day at a time, listen to my intuition and choose the path that feels right at the time. Intuition and inner guidance are very personal. What feels right for you might not feel right for someone else. The outcome of your decisions is irrelevant. Your enjoyment of the journey is what matters.

So, if you still feel that you must do "spiritual" work as part of your soul's purpose, let me ask you, "Who are your clients? Who will you minister to today?" Every person you see in traffic or at the grocery store—every person in your life is your ministry. You send vibrations with your eye contact, your smile, your words, your thoughts, your breath, your emotions. You are a walking lighthouse, beaming out codes and opening portals with just a smile.

CHAPTER 9 ~ Playfulness & Artistic Creation

In every age of reform there has been an upsurge of artistic expression. Through poetry, writing, drawing, painting, and other artistic forms, creative types reflect what is happening in our outer world and reveal what is in our hidden inner world. Artists, shamans, starseeds, healers—all of us lightworkers—are being called to work with our creativity more and more as we raise consciousness on this planet. No matter how much life is changing around us, we can flow in a creative process that brings us into the current moment where we are not focused on what happened yesterday or what tomorrow may bring. Creativity is a form of meditation in which our divine connection is accessed in a very organic manner.

The second chakra represents embodiment, creativity, and birthing. We are birthing a new world! We can use creativity to bridge the sensory body and spiritual essence. Creativity is a big part of our internal guidance system. It brings us into alignment with our intuition and we begin to broadcast or vibrate our energy outward in a manifest form. That may be through cooking, gardening, music, crafting, artwork, or any creative endeavor. It could include starting a podcast or starting a business that helps to promote well-being in the world.

I participated in an Artist Ascension Telesummit hosted by Alexis Cohen in December 2019. Various interviewees shared information about how art works hand in hand with the ascension process. I witnessed people in the group making tremendous strides in self-acceptance as they courageously brought forth their art to be shared in an online community. From there, some launched careers and ministries using their art to monetize their creativity.

We can use creativity artistic expression, vocal expression, dance, and creativity to take us more into the body and out of the programming—especially if we can create in a way that is not contrived and express our authenticity without judging ourselves. If you like to draw, paint, cook, or enjoy any artistic endeavor, allow that to be your gift in the moment. No worries about whether or not it is perfect; just flow with the energy of creation. For example, rather than having a group do movements in which everyone mimics butterflies, allow individuals to choose their own movement they are curious about. Have them ask, "Why am I curious about [unicorns]?" The wounded child becomes the wonder child, ready to explore and adventure.

> "Do you remember when you were small children
> and the world seemed fun and exciting? Be like
> those little children again. Come play with us in the
> wonderland of Matter."
>
> ~ Ken Carey, The Starseed Transmissions

Living from the heart means we do not always need to have the answers in our heads. When people ask me to interpret symbols or light language transmissions I know that person is still viewing life linearly. I encourage them to drop into their heart-space where everything is felt as sensation. Anyone can have a heartfelt knowing of what is being transmitted. There is certainly nothing wrong with using the analytical left side of the brain or to know the interpretation of light language. But trying to give a complex meaning to the syllables and sounds can become too analytical. Like listening to music and wondering what key signature the piece is written in, or predicting the next chord progression, such an approach takes us out of the sensory experience. The two halves of the brain work together, not independently of each other. We need math, science, and other subjects to navigate life and balance our exploration. Harmonizing the left and right brain centers allows us to be creative and process information.

The more we dialogue and name things, the more we take things out of movement. Humans identify with labels that cause us to harshly judge ourselves and one another. We feel that we are not as good as someone else doing a similar endeavor. Perfection is not the goal of being human— experience, curiosity, and exploration is our path to Home.

To fully access inner guidance, one must come to an innocent childlike state where the imprints and programming of childhood can be transfigured. We do this through play, vocalization, and expressing emotions that have been stuffed for years. It takes courage to move past the condemning voice of the distorted personality that causes us to feel inhibited and "less than" others.

To become a child is to see the kingdom of God. In Matthew 18:2-4 of the Bible Jesus called a little child to him and said, "Unless you become like little children, you will never enter the kingdom of heaven. Therefore, whoever takes the lowly position of this child is the greatest in the kingdom of heaven." He was not talking about being childish or selfish, but rather child-like, playful, and innocent (unprogrammed).

As we advance on our journey Home we quickly start to notice when something we say or do is not aligned with love. Rather than reprimanding ourselves for slipping, we can use these "oopsies" as perfect opportunities to lovingly re-direct our thoughts and actions. Self-forgiveness is paramount for moving forward in your exploration. I suppose everyone wishes they had done things differently at some point. We do the best we can with the knowledge and understanding we have at the moment. If we could have done better, we would have. It is good to know that everything we think we did wrong is exactly right for our evolution. Poet Amanda Torroni refers to regrets as "wonderings" because she wonders what would have happened if things had played out differently. Amanda writes, ". . . to name my past decisions as mistakes or regrets is foolish. If I chose something, it was the right choice at the right time. We never purposefully make mistakes; we only call them that in hindsight."

To an artist, the shadows or dark colors are as important as the light ones. Both are necessary to create depth and dimension. The artist decides how dark or how light his or her creation will be. The same is true in our reality. There must be shadows in order to have density and form. Our ascension is moving us into a lighter, less dense form. Therefore, our new creation will look and feel different. Like colored chips inside a kaleidoscope, our multidimensional aspects form different patterns every time there is motion. In life, there is always movement and change. When your life gets shaken, another picture or perspective will be revealed in the rearranged fragments. Another version of yourself may step in with the strength to help you get through a tough situation. Are you amazed at the colors, patterns, and shapes of the multiple versions you see of yourself? Or do you think something must be wrong with your kaleidoscope? Perhaps you shake it harder, hoping to recreate a version of yourself that you liked before or that made you feel safer. Or maybe you avoid shaking things up at all.

Much of life is spent trying to re-navigate or integrate the experiences that occurred during the formative years. It takes courage to allow a transformation process. The process of unifying the personality may take you into deep and unfamiliar places. When dealing with characteristics of the personality, people have told me they think they have demons. If you fear the underworld, demons, death, sickness, or anything else, it will be difficult to feel safe delving deep into the feelings and curiosity of your personality.

> "While there is a deeply ingrained impulse in a human being to uncover the hidden, expose each lie, and cast light on the agendas of inhumane treatment, please know tracking the activities of darkness places the vibrational power of your anchoring of light on pause, in favor of trying to expose a dark agenda that you will willingly align and resonate with."
>
> ~ Matt Kahn

Until you overcome the fear of what lies in the shadows, you will see yourself as separate from these creations. Your attention intensifies the power of whatever it focuses upon. If you believe "demons" are more powerful than you are, this will animate fearful constructs, and seemingly give them a life of their own. They will then confront you and fortify your belief in them because your fear is calling this into your experience. And the longer you fight these mental constructs, the more of a stronghold they take upon your thoughts. I know this personally. If you want to experience or interact with demons, you can create that reality in your thoughts. I know for real that emotions and ego will gladly participate in creating personal mishaps and chaos. Yet, my fight against evil was part of my shamanic training. I did not know what a shaman was in the mid- to late-1990s when I thought spiritual warfare was a noble idea. From that enlightening experience, I learned how energy follows thought and that my thoughts are powerful. This led me to lovingly shift my perspective that literally everything works on behalf of divine will.

> "Yours is not a tame God to be confined in reverent concepts, but a vibrant, playful energy, the very soul and spirit of life! He comes to Earth not to be somber and devout but to dance, sing, and enjoy all that he has created."

> ~ Ken Carey, The Starseed Transmissions

Opposition can be an opportunity for curious exploration. You can feel unpleasant energy without judging it. Step back and observe yourself, your actions, your feelings. From a higher perspective, you can lovingly navigate whatever emotion arises without getting stuck or dragged down by it. Fighting will amplify and extend an unpleasant situation. Running away is a human reaction to anything that seems unusual or scary. Relaxing into the flow or life and surrendering to it is the healing medicine you can obtain without a prescription. When you find yourself acting against something rather than taking time to experience it, notice what is happening.

You can quickly call a ceasefire across the battlefield of your mind as you let go of the need to be anywhere else or feel any way other than how you feel right now. This embraces all aspects of Spirit, body, and personality with kindness, acceptance, and compassion. Some days it is easy to hold space for your feelings and comfort the most repressed parts within you that cry out for love. Other times you may just have to kick and scream at your disappointments and frustration. Each feeling provides a deepening of your relationship with Source.

Even when there is a deep peeling back of the layers to reveal the gifts hidden in your shadows, you may be surprised at how graciously the universe will assist you. When you surrender to a higher consciousness that sees the bigger picture, a deep letting-go may not be as painful as you thought it would be.

We are not casting out the ego—it is part of the personality. We are integrating our fear as we recognize it as part of us that has forgotten its identity. When we are free from fear, even our personality quirks and misbehaviors become humorous. When we can laugh at the way life presents itself and trust that everything is working out for good, we open to new experiences. We become less critical of ourselves or others. We let go of how we think life should or must be as we evolve into a relationship with Spirit. Tell the universe what you want or need, but trust that your prayer will be answered in the way that best supports the evolution of your journey.

Surrender brings playfulness. How do you surrender? By realizing it is all you! Everything is Source and you are part of that mystery. Source is ubiquitous. Therefore, we also exist everywhere simultaneously in multiple realities. We are co-programmers of our reality as we project images and stories and roles. Think of life as a movie or video game. We write the script, cast the characters, create the set, and direct the filming.

When I watch a movie, it is interesting to note how quickly I form a personal connection with the actors. I identify with their feelings and emotions; I cry and laugh along with them even though I am aware it is not real. I tend to love the "good" characters and dislike the "bad" ones. When the movie is over, my dislike for the actor who played the villain has vanished. All the actors were just playing roles. Compare this scenario to your life on the Earth plane in which humans are characters in a non-fiction movie. Life is filled with ups and downs, mixed emotions, good guys, and bad guys which seem to be real.

We have been programmed to live outside of ourselves and allow externals to influence us. For far too long, we have viewed ourselves as we think others see us rather than connecting with who truly we. Our intuitive creativity is a divine link to expressing who we are. Art, dance, music, imagination, and play (especially outdoors) are important ways children express themselves. If we do not give them opportunity to do that, they have no other recourse but to trust in and conform to external directives given by adults and what they read in books or see in movies or video games. If a child is encouraged to follow his or her intuition and explore creative processes and problem-solving, they blossom. They believe in themselves in a way that the programming does not allow.

Living in the moment will assist you in being playful, lighthearted, grateful, and adaptable to change. When things do not go according to plan, we learn to let go of control and roll with the "interruption." We look for ways to approach the situation and choose a response that allows our peaceful state of being to remain steady. That is not to say that we should not feel the emotion of common experiences arising to be healed. We rise above the turbulence by embracing our feelings with openness, maturity, and authenticity. No need to cast them away or ignore them. Instead, surrender into your feelings as a means of exploring your deepest vulnerabilities. This will help you relax in a moment of chaos or when you feel that the Universe is being unfair.

When we love ourselves unconditionally, the unlimited light that we all contain can shine through. That light has been hidden or wrapped up in all the programming and trauma that we have been through. You can tell you are ascending when you begin to play, create, and enjoy freedom the way you did when you were a child. Life becomes simpler as we live in harmony with the present moment. You question less and less.

Our creativity, songs, and soul vibration call us to move past egoic programming and to live as the divine being we know ourselves to be. Our goal is to bring our higher understanding into this level of manifestation. We are being called forward as a channel of high vibrational light. Those who say yes to that light will begin to embark upon a unique, oftentimes intense, path that seems out of the normal. You realize you are in the world, but you are not a prisoner of the world's ideologies or systems.

Our physical body is shifting as the cellular structure adapts to a higher frequency. Those frequencies or bandwidths support us as we embody Spirit and refine our personality. To assist this physical shift, it helps to be fluid and able to flow rather than static. Try adding a playful or creative practice to your response to the next "upset" you encounter.

When I am painting or writing or doing something creative, I connect with myself in a deep way. Many people find doodling to be a creative outlet for expressing without self-judgment. We typically do not expect our doodling to be worthy of hanging in an art gallery. We are not worried about how to perfectly form letters or whether it is grammatically correct. We write non-linearly here and there on the page. What if you were to intentionally doodle? You may be pleasantly surprised by your "ink play." You may begin to write light codes.

When I was first introduced to someone who was writing light codes, my first inclination was to create codes with my mind. I tried to copy what this person was doing or to create symbols like a decoder found on a cereal box! One day, I felt like writing with my nondominant hand. I started at the right side of the page and worked toward the left. I started at the top and wrote downward in a column. I played around in the middle of the page and worked outward because I wanted to get out of the program.

Soon, this practice felt like automatic writing. My hands were being led and I did not know what stroke of the pen was coming next. It got faster and faster to where I decided not to control the motion. I surrendered to the energy moving through me to discover a unique and artistic expression. The more I let go of having my doodling look like something familiar or be like something someone else created, the more natural my writing became.

A person may create codes that look like symbols. Someone else's codes may be more pictorial. Others may seem like mathematical formulas written on a chalk board. Others look like languages. Why do they look so different? Because they are! Musical notes and color spectrums produce different frequencies. A computer may use Java script, CSS, and C++, binary codes, HTML, and other languages. Each programming language has a unique set of keywords that it understands and a special syntax for organizing program instructions.

We can all identify as artists and healers in this new paradigm. People who have never considered themselves artists are now being called to allow mysterious symbols to come forth. It can be a little scary when a lot of power and energy flows through and some strange sounds are transmitted. When faced with fear of your own divine power, ask yourself if you want to continue playing the role of a human overtaken by the mindset that you are powerless, or do you want to open up and be who you are called to be? Sometimes you just have to face the fear and do it anyway. Familiar habits can make us feel safe even if they are not working in our favor. Trust that what is coming through you is Source energy and will never lead you to someplace you are not ready to go. The 5th Element of Unconditional Love is never going to take away your free will. Even when you are channeling like a rolling river, you have the ability to stop the flow if necessary.

Light language telepathically transfers potent information packets that activate an expansion of consciousness. This encoding surpasses human words and intellect. My goal as a celestial shaman is to activate as many people as are ready to focus on inner vibrational frequencies. When I activate others, I remind them of their childlike self—a state of being before the programming and societal imprinting took hold. I ask them to vocalize tones and syllables of any kind they choose. This vibration creates sound waves for the codes of creation to be transmitted to the cells of the physical body, the personal electromagnetic fields or subtle bodies, the DNA, and the crystalline light body.

When you are first activating your light language, it is important to find your voice and make vibrations. They can be OHM, vowel sounds, tongue clicks, whistling, animal noises, singing, humming—however you wish to move vibration into the air waves. This broadcast of sound waves helps open places in the body where restrictions are found. Reconnecting with the playful inner child allows us to experience freedom of expression and undo habits of self-repression. If you sense that you are starting to activate your light language, I encourage you to stop right now and vocalize! At first it may not feel real. If you wonder if what you are speaking is "real" light language and not just jibber-jabber, you are still learning to trust your feelings and intuition. No worries. Keep priming the pump to get the energy flowing through your system. Soon the vector wave will start to vibrate and move through you. When the energy of light language comes through, you will know it. You will feel it. You will be in the still-point where you are flowing energy between the planet and the cosmos. You will have moved beyond analyzing and into sensing.

Enjoy your sounds and the curiosity that arises in this practice. You may become emotional. That is normal. Do not give up if nothing happens the first few times. Your desire to activate is enough to bring it through.

When I use cosmic languages during drum circles, retreats, and online classes, I witness the evident clearing of unresolved energy signatures. We receive downloads of cosmic information by allowing higher/future versions of ourselves to channel through us the codes that can change the world and restore awareness of our divine nature.

Animals almost always respond to light language. If an animal is in the room with a client during a session, most of them will show a keen response when I begin to speak and tone the celestial languages. Those shamans who work with plants and animals will find light language very useful as a tool for connection and healing with the natural world. I was walking in the woods at Big Canoe in the North Georgia Mountains one evening when I came within twenty-five feet of eight deer. They did not run or move away from me as I was singing in light language. One sat on the ground, relaxed and staring at me as if in a trance. I know the animals could feel my energy and were not afraid.

> "In many shamanic societies, if you came to a medicine person complaining of being disheartened, dispirited, or depressed, they would ask one of four questions. When did you stop dancing? When did you stop singing? When did you stop being enchanted by stories? When did you stop finding comfort in the sweet territory of silence? Where we have stopped dancing, singing, being enchanted by stories, or finding comfort in silence is where we have experienced the loss of soul."

~ Angeles Arrien

I hope you have not stopped playing and feeling curious about your world. Some people shut down their playfulness due to some negative comment someone made or some traumatic experience that took the wind out of their sails.

Everyone is creative in some way. We all have something beautiful to share. Your art does not have to be perfect or meet art industry standards. You are already perfect, and whatever you create has value! Bask in that knowledge. Find your piece of the puzzle and share your creativity.

Now get your art supplies, move your body, and practice a fun creation. Be a child again.

CHAPTER 10 ~ Walk-ins

"What are you going to do tomorrow?" I asked Grace. She was integrating and adjusting to the new frequencies of several interdimensional aspects.

She replied, "It depends upon who shows up in my body!" Spoken truly by one who is aware of herself as more than one soul aspect.

Source (All That Is) created the multiverse and populated it with a variety of specialized units of itself, whose purpose is to experience, explore, and evolve within the free-will structure provided on Earth and beyond. Free will means that all entities can choose to serve themselves, serve others, and Source. Beings of pure sentience are known as higher selves, Holy Spirit, or oversouls (monads), which can operate in any frequency band throughout the multiverse. Made in the image of the Creator, these higher selves create smaller units or individualized souls that may take the form of a human or another species on planets, nebulas, and galaxies throughout the multiverse. To enhance the process of exploration, these individuated souls create more souls, which create fractals or fragments that we often refer to as soul aspects. Each fragment or soul aspect has numerous parallel lives playing out simultaneously in various realities, which are occurring all together. These aspects may also create sub-units that can incarnate or operate at lower levels of awareness such as animals, plants, insects, reptiles, minerals, viruses, bacteria, and humans having a smaller percentage of sentience (self-awareness, intelligence, and creativity). Fully sentient beings can evolve faster than lesser sentient ones. All beings are evolving through the frequency bands and will eventually be reintegrated with Source.

It is not uncommon for soul aspects to join an incarnated soul in a physical body. They may walk along together or partner with one another in the short term, long term, or for the entire incarnation. One soul aspect may swap places with another. What we refer to as "walk-ins" are our multidimensional soul aspects joining with or swapping places in various bodies, timelines, or dimensions. This evolutionary process allows us to interact with multiple expressions of ourselves simultaneously. As one 25,920-year cycle ends, things speed up. We are currently evolving thousands of soul aspects and realities simultaneously in a single incarnation/body.

It is possible (though not without the risk of getting stuck) to move from a higher bandwidth down to a lower one. Jesus, though he was in the form of God, did not consider being equal with God something to exploit. Instead, he emptied himself by taking the form of a slave by becoming a human being (Philippians 2:6-7). This indicates that Jesus willingly incarnated into a lower reality to interact with humans. I believe the purpose of this was to show humans how to maintain oneness with Creator while living in a lower vibrational reality. He set an example of how to live in the world with egoic programming and not succumb to believing that was his true identity.

The lower frequencies on Earth have been maintained for the less sentient beings who need to progress through them. Moving up the ascension elevator from a lower bandwidth to a higher one requires a lot of work. One must integrate the shadow side and no longer identify as a victim or perpetrator. Ascending in frequency is a function of evolution. As we master the personality, our spiritual gifts open up. This is when we begin to operate miracles as celestial shamans and help others evolve.

During times of great change like we are now encountering, more evolved Christlike beings are called to Earth to assist those who are evolving at a slower pace. This may be the first time some of you carrying the Christ consciousness have been in a human body on Earth. Everything feels new and different—especially if you walked into your current body as a teenager or adult rather than coming in as a newborn baby. The density of the Earth plane may feel heavy and confining. You may feel like your cosmic parents or teammates dropped you off on Gaia's doorstep and left you to figure it out on your own. It is normal for first-timers to have a strong desire to leave the planet. Bless those of you who are homesick or are struggling to maintain your true identity while in a human form.

We do not have just one expression of ourselves—we are multi-dimensional in the oneness of Source. On Earth, I am a collection of soul aspects operating as a singular incarnated entity known as Yvonne Perry. Thus, I change all the time depending on where I am and who I am with. I imagine you do the same thing. We see ourselves, our lives, and others from a different perspective as we evolve on our path toward Home.

Notice your behavior and feelings as they shift throughout the day. If you pay attention to yourself when you are in public, you may notice that different parts of your personality come forward or step back depending upon the circumstances and what you want to convey or accomplish. You may feel or act differently alone than you do in a crowd. You may become more playful around children and act more sophisticated around corporate executives. That is because the field is different. After a hardship is over, you may say, "I feel like my old self again." Who were you in the meanwhile? You adapt by presenting different aspects of yourself. This is how you utilize the entirety of your personality in your spiritual database. Your spiritual database encompasses every aspect of who you need to be while you are here on Earth. There is no need to attach to any of them. These are roles we play in the big movie of life.

Some believe that a "walk-in" is the soul of another person. While we may be different from others, we are all variations of Source having a spirit-in-matter experience. All my walk-ins have been individualized soul aspects sent from my higher self to join this body for a season or a moment. Even the walk-ins that completely changed my life and personality are fractal units of my oversoul. I have had soul aspects return for visits from time to time. Some have integrated/merged so well they no longer feel like a different aspect.

The beginning and the end of our journey are in the same place. Our perception determines our reality. If we are all a part of the Source, expressing a unique experience on Earth, then it makes sense that we would have different parts of our God-self in the same body at the same time. Or, that there may be a rotation so that multiple soul aspects can explore being a human.

Spirit is light that acts as consciousness. Light can be observed as a wave (spirit) or a particle (matter) that operates on a quantum level which cannot be seen with the naked eye. Consciousness can beam itself into a body or form designed to hold such energy. It can move from place to place and randomly appear differently.

When a wave of light consciousness (Spirit) finds a body/form whose frequency matches its reality and is energetically compatible, it may transfer to, swap places with, or blend (cohabitate) with the consciousness already in that body. Earth technology and understanding of the invisible realms is behind by millennia compared to technology used by beings on planets in other star systems or universes. However, scientists are beginning to explore reality from a metaphysical perspective which is opening their understanding of how Spirit and science are interwoven.

"Things behave very strangely at the quantum level. We cannot see them with the unaided eye, of course, but we can detect them through instrumentation, and their properties and behavior can be described mathematically by a formula called the "wave function." Under certain circumstances the wave function divides into two or more pairs or branches, each with its own consequences. Each of these branches represents a potential future or a potential version of reality. When observed, only one of these branches is perceived; that is, only one of the potential futures becomes the actual perceived present."

~ William Meacham

My interview with Hope Gorman was scheduled months before I knew all the changes that I would be facing at the end of October. The time for the interview came right in the middle of packing boxes, closing real estate deals, loading PODS and trucks while my divorce was in process. The movers had just about emptied the house and I sat in my office with my laptop on the floor.

Hope started out by asking me, "Where do walk-ins come from?"

My answer surprised me "Where do any of us come from? Do we come from Source? Other planets, dimensions, or galaxies? Yes, and yes, and yes."

I have clarified and expanded my thoughts on this pertinent question since then. Celestial shamans are sovereign souls who come from other star/solar systems before incarnating on Earth. Once we enter a body, we are introduced to the force field of Earth and the quirks of an ego/personality.

In the traditional understanding of reincarnation, the body would die in order to release the Spirit. Then, the Spirit could re-enter the Earth realm in a new body—that of a baby. The walk-in is like reincarnation on steroids! Many lifetimes are being lived or completed in one incarnation/body. As our parallel lives begin to integrate, this process will continue to move faster until complete unity is achieved. Have you been aware of more than one expression of your holographic parts in your body at a time?

Every human baby has a Spirit animating it within the womb. The natal (born-in) aspect may not be a permanent inhabitant. It may accomplish its integration goals while the body is still viable. Rather than having the body die, another aspect of consciousness may walk in and animate the child, teen, or adult body. This can create big changes in life—especially if there is a wide enough variation in the bandwidth between the natal aspect and the walk-in aspect.

What triggers a walk-in? Sometimes the quantum leap seems random and is not proceeded by any perceivable circumstances. This is because the Earth is receiving rays of light to help all beings on the planet to ascend. However, the most common triggers are a near-death experience, surgery, head injury, emotional overload, Reiki treatments, light language transmissions, and participation in plant ceremonies, being in a gathering of high energy souls, or receiving energy work.

Over the centuries of our evolutionary process we have defined certain experiences with the terminology we had available or that was accepted and understood by most people. In my first book, Walk-ins Among Us, I shared what I knew at the time about soul swaps, braids, and placeholders. Afterward, I got a lot of requests from people who wanted me to facilitate a walk-in for them. To me, that seemed like an escape from dealing with the mess the personality had created. No matter what aspect is in the body, someone has to do the hard task of mastering the personality. I have learned much more since that book came out in 2013. I now see the walk-in or soul integration process as an organic part of the overall purification or metamorphosis of coming into the 6th Element of Home.

I believe that each person has the responsibility to do their own ascension work, and that we should interfere as little as possible in another person's process. I do not suggest you go around asking people if they have had a walk-in. However, "walk-in" is becoming a common term in spiritual circles. It is possible that someone may ask you to help them as a spiritual rebirth doula or a reincarnation/walk-in assistant. Before you try to initiate a walk-in please use keen discernment to determine if this is your work to do and if your help is in the client's best interest. If you are in a spiritual gathering and notice that someone is experiencing a re-birth, simply hold loving space and let Spirit do the work.

The born-again or walk-in process is reincarnation in the same body, as indicated in John 3:1-8 of the New Century Version of the Bible, which I quote here.

There was a man named Nicodemus who was one of the Pharisees and an important Jewish leader. One night Nicodemus came to Jesus and said, "Teacher, we know you are a teacher sent from God, because no one can do the miracles you do unless God is with him."

Jesus answered, "I tell you the truth, unless you are born again, you cannot be in God's kingdom."

Nicodemus said, "But if a person is already old, how can he be born again? He cannot enter his mother's womb again. So how can a person be born a second time?"

But Jesus answered, "I tell you the truth, unless you are born from water and the Spirit, you cannot enter God's kingdom. Human life comes from human parents, but spiritual life comes from the Spirit. Don't be surprised when I tell you, 'You must all be born again.' The wind blows where it wants to and you hear the sound of it, but you don't know where the wind comes from or where it is going. It is the same with every person who is born from the Spirit."

From this passage, we can conclude that the oversoul or spirit decides when or if a walk-in should take place. We do not have to request it or try to make it happen.

Birth and death can be life-changing for everyone involved. A sudden shift in consciousness can influence the dissolving of relationships. The vibration of the walk-in may not be compatible with the partner or acquaintances of the walk-out. This could be a good thing, especially if there was an abusive situation and the former soul was not able to find the strength to depart from that relationship. Many walk-ins initiate a change of career or create new acquaintances and connections with other embodied soul family members. Some change their name legally or prefer to be called by a name that better resonates with the new energy. The soul team is concerned, not only with the soul aspects, but with the body that anchors a portal to Earth and gives access to the celestial team. If the team needs to change the latitude and longitude of the anchor point of the human portal, the walk-in may feel the need to change residences to live in a different city, state, or country.

What is it like to have a sudden shift such as a walk-in? One client gave me an update about what happened after our session in April 2020. She wrote:

"Yesterday my whole entire reality was shattered... all illusions broken... the veil lifted... saw every single experience as just an experience for learning and growth. What seemed negative was no longer perceived the same way... everything was for a purpose. Trauma is only to be used as a "catalyst" for change, growth, and triggering awakening. I felt a newfound forgiveness and love for every single person and event of the past. I made peace with the past and every soul who was used for my experiences and life lessons. I felt like I officially felt true peace in my heart and soul... not just for me, but every member of my soul family. Suddenly, I felt dizzy, I couldn't stand, my body began shaking uncontrollably, a power so great that I came out of my body and lost consciousness... once I became conscious, my ears rang extremely loud for minutes, an energy burst from my heart so powerful that I let out the biggest cry for all of humanity... then I stood up, and my first words that came from my soul as tears ran down my face were "My God... I was blind, but now I see... thank you for setting me free... thank you for showing me truth... I am Starlight Rose." Since then, I began speaking a light language that I never heard before or understand, but I still speak it daily.

My fiancé has been writing light language and speaking ever since hearing me and listening to your meditations. I was shown a review of my previous life from a higher perspective. I saw myself as the higher consciousness guiding my human self. I was able to see her for what she couldn't see herself to be. I was so proud of her! If only she could've believed in herself more... she had no idea how powerful she was! She had no idea that every negative experience and trauma was only to "trigger" and "activate" her power that she believed was gone. Mistakes were only made when she didn't follow her heart. Since I only know how to lead with my heart, many changes took place overnight. I even changed my number, have no contact with anyone she previously had connections with, and do not plan to return to her previous job which was extremely toxic and damaging to her health in ways she felt, but didn't fully realize. So, it is time for big changes!"

~ Leticia

Since there are different types of walk-ins, I am certain that everyone who is awakening will have some type of mystical experience that they may not be able to logically explain. Whether the in-born (natal) aspect of consciousness leaves and is replaced by another, or if a secondary aspect comes in and shares the same body, these mystical experiences can be called walk-ins or being "born again." Some people call them kundalini awakenings due to the rapturous bliss they encounter with the experience. Afterward, people feel different. They usually have a better perspective on life, and are able to handle situations with a calmer approach.

A higher aspect or future self may come to help with a life transition. A placeholder may animate the body and transmute detrimental emotional signatures during a transition period while a walk-out aspect recuperates or moves to another reality. During a placeholder phase, there is a waiting period during which a decision is made regarding whether the placeholder needs to stay longer or if it is possible for the previous soul aspect to return. If the aspect does return but still has a strong desire to leave, the placeholder may stay longer, or another walk-in may occur. Rather than leaving, we are seeing more parts and pieces (soul aspects) coming and staying as we return to wholeness. Leticia also said:

> "I've been doing RBQT-18" everyday which has my body feeling more aligned with me, a sense of confidence, feeling empowered. It also feels like it's going through another shift, as if another aspect is trying to emerge. So that is triggering symptoms. My body feels overstimulated, feels like it's trying to adjust to energies from other galaxies and all over the place multidimensionally, on top of the ones I've

already been working on grounding, so it's been very intense!"

Having multiple aspects in the body simultaneously can create some scary feelings, even for those who have been doing shadow work to integrate soul aspects. Fragmented soul aspects may appear in such a state of disarray energetically/emotionally that letting go and allowing the walk-in is difficult. At times, the ego personality refuses to step aside and let the higher soul aspect do what it needs to do. To allow the ego to continue its rebellious behavior could result in body death. The incoming soul calms the fragmented aspect(s) with something like an anesthesia, which puts the ego it into a dissociative state. I have known people to have shifts that put them in a blissful state for days, weeks, or even months, and then the state of bliss dissipates when the work on the physical body is complete.

When there is a dramatic vibrational difference in aspects, everything may feel new to the incoming aspect. Some walk-ins coming into human bodies have never had a lifetime on Earth. They are somewhat stunned by finding themselves in a dense state where everything is slower and heavy. There is no baby stage to help the newbie slowly adjust. They are expected to make decisions, drive a car, and accept adult responsibilities when all they want to do is explore how many fingers they have on each hand! They touch, smell, taste, listen, and look around with awe and wonder. Words feel strange and inadequate to those who were accustomed to communicating telepathically. Some experience sensory overload as they adjust to this new life.

Being conscious of the walk-in/non-death reincarnation process can help to relieve anxiety and resistance, which allows aspect integration to unfold easier and quicker. Take things one day at a time and be present in the body. Acknowledge the feelings that are flowing through as part of the adjustment phase. Be curious about life. There is nothing wrong with you or what you are experiencing—nothing needs to be fixed.

Twin Flames and Soul Mates

Your eyes lock in a flirtatious way that brings a sense of excitement. It feels like you have always known each other. There is an unexplainable vibratory connection between you. The conversation flows effortlessly. Eureka! "He's my twin flame!" you announce to yourself and your Facebook friends.

It is easy to confuse a twin flame spark for infatuation. I do not feel that I am half of anyone else or that half of my soul is missing. I do sense that there is a duplicate version of my soul's personal energy signature. This duplicated frequency can animate two bodies at once. I have met my twin self in the body of other persons three separate times. Even though their physical bodies looked very different from mine, their energy felt overwhelmingly familiar and the connection I had with them (even though only briefly) was intense. I will mention more about this in the section about skin-walking.

Naturally, you are going to resonate with some people more than you do with others. The vibration of the personality of some people is more complimentary or compatible with yours. A new person may come to you as a catalyst to help you make changes in life, perhaps in your relationship with your current partner. It could be lust and infatuation. How do you know? The same way you know the difference in being Spirit-led and personality-led. You aim to allow Spirit to be in control all the time.

"A soulmate's purpose is to shake you up, tear apart your ego a little bit, show you your obstacles and addictions, break your heart open so new light can get in, make you so desperate and out of control that you have to transform your life."

~ Elizabeth Gilbert (Eat, Pray, Love)

Our personalities are expressed differently because we live through filters of individual and joined experiences. Much of the discord encountered in relationships is due to distractions that pull us out of sync with our personal rhythm. Living from a place of self-love and acceptance makes it easier to not project needs and expectations on another person.

It may feel like you have known them in a past life, and that is likely the case. There may be a soul memory, a feeling or connection with them on an etheric level. When you say that you are "vibing" with your soul mate, it is because your codes are a vibrational match for one another. When you come into contact with somebody who is vibrating at the old paradigm it can feel off-putting or even eerie.

Most so-called twin flame relationships only last until the "hotness" or new relationship energy wears off and real life begins. One partner will either leave or pull away when the purpose of the relationship is finished. Some do not end well—especially if one partner is not willing to integrate his or her unresolved emotions. The impact is so strong, it will leave an impression that is hard to forget.

From my work with clients and my personal experience, the twin flame journey that people talk about is rarely one of romance or glamour as has been portrayed. Instead, it is a triggering relationship that unearths the shadow side of each person.

Every person has personality quirks that he or she may or may not be integrating with body and Spirit. That can cause emotional pain—especially if it is triggering unresolved childhood issues for either person. It is common for one partner to be doing their shadow work while the other one resists change. The "evolving" partner urges their partner to wake up spiritually. Naturally, this creates tension in the relationship, and yet the disenchanted partners often stay together in hopes that their partner will change. Thus, a trauma bond is formed (financial dependence, fear of losing children, not wanting to be alone, etc.) that prevents a partner from physically leaving, even though their heart (or the heart of their partner) may have left many months or years prior. Staying together out of fear is not an expression of unconditional love.

I believe every soul is a vital part of Source. We live under the illusion of separation as we express individual personalities. When one partner is not attempting to master his or her emotional energy, and the other partner more frequently lives in alignment with the higher self, the two are "unequally yoked," as the Bible calls it. Your partner may be able to align with some of your frequencies, some of the time, but when your vibrational frequencies do not align well, you may feel more at ease and peaceful when that person is not around you. Do not allow someone to jam up your gears and take your power away. If someone is not part of the solution, they may be part of the problem.

> "It is no secret that, for many, intimate relationship is one of the great amplifiers of the unlived life. We can count on our partners and close friends to

relentlessly illuminate everything that remains unresolved within us. Not because they have some agenda to do so, but simply by the nature of the vessel that forms when we allow another to truly matter.

"There is nothing like a close relationship to illuminate the orphaned emotions, beliefs, and vulnerable parts of ourselves that have lost their way in the tangle of somatic and psychic pathways. It can be a revelation to see how we attract and are attracted to those aspects and qualities in the other that we have disowned in ourselves."

~ Matt Licata

I think "twin ray" is a better term for what we are seeking in another person to remind us that we are already whole. The twin ray is the flow of Source energy within us—the sacred union we have with our higher selves. It exists in every person. Our Earth traumas, programming, and experiences keep it well hidden as we seek connection with others. Twin ray marriage with Source is experienced within the still-point of our hearts. This "God" self is perfect, and it is you! It will never let you down, try to control you, reject you for the decisions you make, or judge you for any reason.

That said, it sure feels good when an emotionally mature person who is a vibrational match shares that union with you!

What is a Skin-Walker?

"My twin flame is coming back as a walk-in so we can be together again. When he comes back, will he remember being who he was in this last life? I would love for him to remember our life together and know who I am to him."

I am asked this quite often.

At first, these statements and questions sounded like a wish that no genie could fulfill. As I began to understand how Source is present in body, Spirit, and personality, I took a different view. Perhaps those who sense that their twin flame is coming back in another body are looking in the wrong place. Perhaps the merged walk-in is happening within their own body, rather than in a separate identity. Could this be why it feels like part of the deceased loved one is inside you? The two identities merged into one—momentarily or for the long term.

From what I understand, the essence/consciousness of the discarnate beloved magnetically attaches to the neural transmitters in the brain and communicates through the voice and behaviors of the host person. You may recognize your beloved in another person through the words or mannerisms that remind you of your beloved. The host's personality is also being expressed, making it difficult to recognize your beloved. The host may feel blissful or expanded during the blend and may not realize they are experiencing a skin-walker.

There can be a strong kundalini energy during a skin-walking experience—both for you and the host. This surge has been interpreted as a twin flame or love affair, but the purpose of this union is not necessarily for sex in the physical sense. However, chakra or body orgasm in this heightened state can feel incredibly better than any physical union you may have encountered.

My grandmother's essence/spirit walked through my body when her physical body died. Blissful does not even begin to describe the feeling. It lasted for days while I spent time with family following her death. She gave me the grace to play and sing at her funeral like she had requested years prior. We are now blended in my heart space, where she is more than a memory. She is an aliveness, a presence which reminds me that we are of the same oversoul, or monad. Whenever I see mourning doves or hear them cooing I am reminded of the wonderful times we had together in separate bodies before she merged with me. Ah, this morning there were doves at my bird feeder as I typed this section. As I pause and tap in, I can feel her sweet love flowing through me.

Counterparts of your multidimensional spirit exists in simultaneous lifetimes. Skin-walking happens in an exceptionally beautiful way that allows a beloved or companion consciousness to interact with you through the body of another person who holds a similar vibrational resonance. This "overshadowing" or body-sharing is a deep connection with your own vibration in higher dimensions. The higher dimensional energy can drop by for a visit or walk through your own body. The merge may last for months or minutes. It can feel like the part of you that you see in the mirror walked out of the mirror and into your body.

The consciousness of the primary soul essence in the host body does not need to step aside for this purpose. A beloved counterpart of my vibrational expression from another dimension interacted with me in this dimension through the body of a young man I encountered in Denver 2016. I was grieving and felt empty at the time, having lost contact with another beloved counterpart of myself, a person with whom I had been very close for more than a year.

The encounter with the man in Denver occurred when we were in a class about connecting with others through the eyes. As he and I gazed into the being of one another, something happened. It brought us both to our knees in tears and overwhelming bliss. We could hardly stand up because the energy we were sharing was so powerful. I knew what was happening because a few weeks earlier my guidance had told me that I would "meet my beloved" again while I was in Denver. I had forgotten about it until we were face to face.

As this young man and I were sobbing in one another's arms, I asked him, "Are you him?" He replied, "Yes!" but later said he did not know why he said that. He did not even know what I meant by that, just that it felt like truth. Naturally, he had a lot of questions about what was happening. So, we met the next day to talk after we had each had time to recover from the intense energy rush we experienced.

CHAPTER 11 ~ Relationships in the New Paradigm

The typical American family after World War II shared common traits. A dominating male father figure lorded over a subservient female mother and several children from whom strict obedience was required. Extended family usually lived close by and made a major contribution toward the preservation of and adherence to these roles. Society was supplied with communal organizations, which reinforced the family values; and religious beliefs dictated monogamy, shunned divorce, bullied gays, and labeled anyone who strayed from these expectations as unfit to raise children or to take public leadership roles. Some were rejected by family for marrying someone of a different skin color.

Overall, as a society, we are still trying to adhere to the principles of how to be a family and have relationships that seemed to work years ago. As a result, extended families are disjointed, and more children are growing up in dysfunctional homes. I believe it is better for a child to be raised in a single parent home than to be subjected to abusive, irrational, emotionally volatile, and immature behavior from adult caregivers. Things have to change and, indeed, the shift we currently in requires it. The true and undistorted Divine Mother Sophia is returning to her rightful place!.

It is no longer the desire or need of some couples or families to be headed by one male and one female. In spite of public ridicule, assault, and not being allowed to legally adopt children, same-gender couples and polyamorous triads/quads are capable of creating a very nurturing environment where well-adjusted children flourish and excel.

> People take different roads seeking fulfillment and happiness. Just because they are not on your road doesn't mean they've gotten lost.
>
> ~ H. Jackson Brown, Jr., Life's Little Instruction Book

If you have ever been in love with someone you were not supposed to be in love with, you are fully aware that the heart knows no demographics. Age, gender, appearance, race, religion, etc. is not part of the equation or operation of the Spirit. Those limitations are mental programs our personality has come to accept. Prejudice is a learned behavior. It can be unlearned as well.

Studies show that as many as seventy percent of marriages will experience "cheating" at least once during their existence. Some very loving people may feel guilty or condemned because they have a history of not being able to keep wedding vows that require them to forsake all others. Many are uncomfortable committing to a relationship that restricts them emotionally and sexually.

Monogamy may give people a false sense of security that their partner will always be with them and no one else. Perhaps they believe that they will never be tempted or that if they are tempted to enjoy fulfilling relationships and share their body with another, they will not succumb. We want to control our future, but in reality we never have the guarantee that the person we are with now will continue to be with us, regardless of how many vows or promises we make to one another.

It is normal to be attracted to or desire intimacy with more than one person. Repressing passion and attraction is not going to make it go away. It will probably only make it increase. When feelings are pressed down and denied, they build up pressure that can explode at an inopportune moment. Religion has taught us to deny our "carnal" pleasures and to deal with "evil" by casting it out or pushing it down. Religious leaders who pretend to be holy without doing their shadow work have been known to sexuality abuse innocent people.

Monogamy is not the problem. Sex is not the problem. The problem with relationships is emotional immaturity and unresolved karmic patterns such as jealousy, judgment, insecurity, lack of self-worth, fear of loss/abandonment, and other issues that need to be transcended.

We know that our culture is not a reliable source of truth, yet some people try to live by its code, and attempt to force their standards of morality onto others by creating legislation that prohibits freedom of personal choice. Not conforming to societal norms and expectations is not a character flaw. It is a matter of owning your power and honoring your truth. Letting go of the need to control another person or allowing someone else to control you is part of your evolutionary destiny.

It is sad when we allow the B.S. (belief systems) of unenlightened others to distract us and cause us to act out of alignment with our own truth. Buying into their old programing is like trying to put a floppy disc into a USB port of your computer. It simply does not fit. Most who are drawn to a book like this have felt like misfits all their lives. They are accustomed to being different, but that does not mean they like being thought of as strange or weird. Being a way-shower does not always make one popular for the best reasons.

As humans continue to evolve, we are going to see more people identifying with being androgynous, bisexual, transgendered, gay, lesbian, and even nonsexual. In higher realms, beings to do not take on the separated identity of male and female. As we come into wholeness, we will begin to display harmonized masculine and feminine characteristics. With emotional maturity our culture will become more accepting of these lifestyles and will embrace biracial families as a valuable part of our society. The dividing lines between rich and poor, celebrities and fans, and other demographic factors will blur more and more as each person honors their own unique expression of Source.

The 5th Element

As a society, we have been perpetuating distortion in love and sexuality for eons. Throughout history, religion and culture have taught us that the body is bad and cannot be loved or appreciated. Some doctrines and religions shame us, cause us to doubt our divinity, and teach us to live in fear. The Bible suggests that the body's innate longing for connection with higher realms through sexual pleasure was evil. Nothing could be farther from the truth! Our connection to Source is a very sensory experience. The gateway to higher realms through sexual pleasure is well known and practiced in some cultures.

Intimacy is what we truly long for. To love and be loved. To know and be known. To accept and be accepted. The 5th

Element is holy compassion and unconditional love, not the Hollywood version of love, which is nothing more than lust and perversion. As we come into alignment with the 5th Element we may notice our relationships changing. Some that we thought would last forever suddenly end. Some that were out of sync vibrationally (unequally yoked) transform to support the mission of both partners. People who were always straight may begin to realize they are attracted to their same gender.

If we are to grow and heal from our misguided programming, we must allow the shifts to occur within us and our relationships. This requires detaching from outcomes, letting go of codependent behavior, setting healthy boundaries, and speaking our truth. Similar to the way children stop believing in Santa Claus, the collective human belief system is changing as we are awakening to higher realms of consciousness.

If you are in a monogamous marriage with a jealous partner, you may find that it prevents, or slows down, your spiritual development. You may have to decide if staying is in your best interest, or if leaving will provide better opportunities for your spiritual growth. You could try to shift your relationship into a more inclusive one that maintains trust and intimacy.

I have little experience with polyamory, other than the heartbreak that loving and wanting to be intimate with more than one person at a time has brought me. During each of my two long-term marriages, I met people who positively influenced my spiritual growth and met my emotional needs. Though I refrained from sexual exploration with these men due to the monogamous vows I had made, my friendships with them triggered jealousy in my husband(s). The codependent part of my programming urged me to keep peace and not rock the boat. Repeatedly, I had to stop my interaction and curb the joy I was experiencing in order put my partner at ease. I knew that if I could get him calmed down, I could continue to move forward in my exploration with what the Universe was offering me and teaching me.

Going into a relationship with honesty and freedom up front is easier than shifting a monogamous relationship after committing to life-long vows that much of the married population is not keeping. I encountered panic attacks when I began trying to shift my monogamous marriage into a more inclusive one. I felt wrong for wanting more. I did not want to lose the man I loved and had a good life with. By the same token, I did not want to deny myself the pleasure and potential growth that I knew could come from being intimate with another person. I wanted happiness and more love in my life without having to sacrifice the love I already had.

> "Why does it have to be wrong or right?
> Why does it have to be one way or the other?
> Won't somebody please, please tell me
> Why does it have to be black or white?
> Why do we have to hurt one to love another?
> Oh, tell me why, why does it have to be?"

> ~ Randy Sharp, Donny R. Lowery

Ascension is about becoming real and authentic. Dealing with the part of us that we feel ashamed of or that is not accepted by our family, friends, coworkers, employers, church, or spouse is part of the Homecoming process. Relationships in the new paradigm are honest ones. Hiding our love "affairs" is a deceptive way of enjoying emotional connection and sexual pleasure with another person. These encounters can serve to awaken us to our soul's true desires. They can catapult us out of a stagnant relationship. They can impose change upon our lives. But when hidden affairs are uncovered, there are unpleasant consequences. The person who has been cheated on feels betrayed and the trust they had for their partner is broken. Deception and consequential betrayal would not be a factor if relationships began with the freedom to explore and grow as needed.

"Authenticity is a vital part of our experience as spirit beings having a human incarnation. Whenever we are out of sync with our truth, we are miserable. Your inner strength allows you to operate powerfully in this world. Spiritual opening is a wonderful, loving experience. But, it comes with a few surprises."

~ Jamye Price

"It is sad to belong to someone else when the right one comes along" does not apply when your intimate partner(s) are practicing the art of inclusive honest love for self and others. We do not stop loving our firstborn child when we have a second or third child. We do not stop loving our parents when we get married or move away. We love our friends, coworkers, and total strangers because as beings of divine light, we are love. Whomever you feel drawn to share love with is the person who needs it most at that moment. Love the one you are with and never lose sight of the overall picture of expanding love.

There is a difference between having sex and making love. Lovemaking is a tool for connecting spiritually that allows us to share positive touch with others. It does not involve sex, but it does create intimate bonds. Lovemaking is about feeling energy and connecting our hearts spiritually and emotionally. Therefore, we can make love to our children, parents, friends, and animals through gazing into one another's eyes, holding a long hug, giving back rubs, holding hands, or a sweet smile that says "I love and accept you" for who you are. This produces oxytocin, which heals the body as it touches deep places in the emotions.

Like the man in Denver and the way my grandmother's energy moves through me, lovemaking can be done with anyone aligned with love. There have been times when I am in session with a client and my heart is flooded with ecstatic love for them. I continue to feel that beautiful connection even after the session is over. I have even felt this for people I am in line with at a checkout counter or when I am talking on the phone with someone from a service provider company. Think of someone right now who brings you a warm feeling of love and connection. Feel that and expand it. This will be the norm in the new world that we are creating.

Integrating Higher Self (Spirit) into the body and personality helps us hold a consistent field of light. This field attracts others to us, and we are attracted to others who hold a similar vibrational field. Our interactions with vibrationally matched people can create some intimate bonds that we have not given ourselves permission to enjoy. One purpose of this book is to shine a light in the darkness so we can see our own faces and not turn away from what we see in the mirror. Love releases things that are not authentic in order to raise our level of consciousness.

During the sacred reset that the COVID-19 offers humanity, people are walking the streets wearing masks. The symbolism is clear, we have been wearing a façade that keeps us from presenting our true selves and full face to the world. The masks are coming off as we enter the new world with transparency that allows us all to be and express the love of God to all of creation.

Having the ability to love, be emotionally intimate, and sometimes sexual in a relationship with more than one person at a time is a non-possessive, non-controlling way to give and receive love. Humans are seeking love and spiritual connection with one another and with Spirit. Sex is only one part of that quest.

Let me be clear that I do not advocate a rampant and dangerous practice where drunken one-night stands and unsafe sex are the norm. We have enough empty, hollow, and unfulfilling relationships already. We have enough escape mechanisms that keep us from facing unresolved pain.

Feeling personally secure means knowing that your love for your partner is not threatened by the presence of more love from someone else. Unconditional love is the absence of jealously or control and allows for curious expression of free will. Honesty with oneself and significant others requires boundaries and maturity to avoid setting yourself up to be a victim or perpetrator of betrayal.

Deciding on boundaries is part of negotiating the terms for any intimate relationship. Some people are terribly uncomfortable with anything other than monogamy in an intimate relationship. A poly relationship requires a level of emotional maturity that is above and beyond what most people can manage. If you think dealing with one intimate relationship is hard, try having a spouse and a girlfriend or boyfriend. Polyamory is an expansive and gut-level honest type of love. In a monogamous relationship it is easier to hide, cover up, or ignore problems, but when a couple starts involving others in their relationship, many of those problems will come to the surface, including addictions or unhealed childhood or past relationship issues. Why? Because it is basically a multiple marriage in which everything multiplies—joy, love, companionship, and sex, as well as pain, conflict, co-dependencies, escape patterns, etc. This lifestyle is not for everyone, and I am not suggesting you change what is working for you. I am asking that we honor the lifestyles and choices others have made for themselves,

Communication is important in any relationship, but especially so in intimate or open relationships.

Here is Joanna's view on polyamory:

"Polyamory has come into my field many times in the past several years. My past relationships in monogamy were very controlling and possessive. I always felt trapped in monogamy. I think this is the reason I was attracted to polyamorous men. I did not know they were polyamorous. They were not up front about it from the start until we created an intimate connection. This was painful for me, because of the way I perceived our connection, and finding out there was a lack of honesty. This was also painful for them because of my rejection to having them reveal who they were. Even though I am attracted to freedom, I have a deep desire for strong spiritual union. I have not been able to experience that with more than one person at the same time. I feel the energy is scattered when I try and focus on different people at the same time. So, I have some work in finding a balance. Also, I cannot seem to fully step into the idea of polyamory due to the way I perceive and feel energetic chords. Being in a polyamorous relationship feels like being chorded to many people, which can feel chaotic. So,

I find myself alone. Not wanting to be controlled by monogamy, and not wanting to be chorded in polyamory. I am hoping to find a balance someday soon."

When facing challenges in an intimate relationship, a fortifying person may appear in your life as a counterbalance. This catalyst person will shake things up a bit. I have served others in this role several times. I have also been supported by this kind of game-changer when my marriages needed transformation. A higher aspect of our Spirit orchestrates these perfectly timed meetings that provide heart connection with another person. The purpose is to activate us or awaken us personally. They can also serve as a wake-up call for a failing relationship and give it a chance to shift it and ourselves to a new level.

A new person may spark aliveness that raises our serotonin, dopamine, and oxytocin levels. These chemicals give us the courage to do things we would not normally do. It could help us make changes in our current relationship that has run our batteries down. We may not realize how depleted or dormant our long-term relationship is until this new energy enters the scene. This relationship can be a catalyst for positive change and help us face a difficult situation. It brings a need for honest communication. These "extra" relationships need not be hidden or repressed. Nor do they have to replace the love we have with our current partner. The problem with ending the current relationship is obvious—you stand to lose someone you love. Your financial security may take a hit. There may be children involved.

The catalyst relationship may provide the oil needed to loosen stagnant energy in your ascension process, open your eyes to new possibilities, and bring a fresh perspective to life. Catalyst relationships are divine appointments—not typically someone you meet after having too many drinks in a bar. They rarely last long term, but if they do, it is a plus. While the person may not be the destination, they may be the starting point for helping you open more fully to love.

When you meet a new person and realize that they are about to play a catalyst role in your life or you are about to play a catalyst role in theirs, you may want to have a heart-to-heart talk upfront so no one gets their feelings hurt when things start to demagnetize. After a while, a catalyst relationship will encounter a falling away in which each person will begin to integrate the experience without the other.

Having an activation person in your life is likely going to challenge your current relationship. There is a benefit to this. Your current partner gets an opportunity to heal any abandonment and betrayal issues or childhood traumas. He or she may have to deal with jealousy, anger, or feelings of unworthiness, not being good enough, or fear that you are about to leave.

We need interaction with like-minded people. When we find our tribe and establish deep friendships, it can be really fulfilling. When someone comes into your life and they are in a state of change, they may not stay for long. The spark was there to facilitate change. Once that happens, the need for the relationship may be over. Like training wheels on a bike, you do not need them once you learn to ride. But letting them go from your life can be painful and scary.

"People come and go in our lives. Sometimes they keep journeying with us, and at other times, they leave to find their own distant shores. Sometimes it is sudden, and at other times, a known and inevitable consequence unfolding. Sometimes they say goodbye, thank you, I Love You - and at other times, nothing at all.

And sometimes ... they come back. Taking a moment to revere those who are in our lives, and energy they bring to us, and we to them, is something I'd recommend as a daily practice. Or simply, whenever it feels right."

~ Bairavee Balasubramaniam

People come into our lives to teach us what we need to learn. They challenge us to look inward and change our emotional patterns. If we are not ready to learn, the same lesson will repeat itself to reveal and heal unresolved issues on all levels, timelines, and dimensions.

When a relationship ends, we may feel empty or betrayed. We may believe that life will never be the same. Truth is we are simply in between the version of ourselves who fell for this person and the version who will rise up in their absence. Things have shifted and so have we.

Focus on the gifts that the friendship brought and send thanks to the individual who helped you overcome the obstacle you chose to work with. Once a relationship has ended and growth is attained, you can walk away feeling appreciation for the efforts each of you made. Divine purpose has been served and it is time to let go.

This "afterbirth" can bring up all kinds of unresolved issues or hurts from your past. Herein, is another opportunity for you to heal. Remember this is a process so be gentle with yourself.

The emptiness in your heart signifies the need to nurture yourself, take time to recover, and plug back into what brings you joy. At night before you sleep, offer a prayer such as "Whatever is left unresolved between me and _____ let it be healed/resolved during the dream time on all levels, dimensions, and lifetimes."

"The practice of rupture and repair is a lost art in our world. Through the reparation of neural pathways and planting seeds of wisdom and compassion, it reveals that relationships of vast depth and meaning are not free of conflict, but those where working through conflict is embraced as path, as unique and powerful temples of purification, love, and healing."

~ Matt Licata

CHAPTER 12 ~ Working with Other Celestial Shamans

When we crave connection and emotional support, it is helpful to be with people who are positively navigating similar emotions and can offer support. I think the toughest part for most people during the coronavirus pandemic has been to avoid physical contact with one another. Thankfully, we have technology that allows us to connect virtually. If that technology were to no longer be available, I wonder if we would still be able to communicate. Restoring our telepathic skills is important during this shift in human consciousness.

Since moving to my new place right before the 2019 holidays, I have enjoyed a simpler life. Rather than having to do anything, I get to engage in creative activities and do only what life is asking of me. That may be as simple as brushing my teeth, cleaning the house, typing this book, working in my yard, or eating lunch. The challenge is to be here now and express gratitude even when I may not feel up to par, or when I am calming fear or resistance coming up in my personality.

Our communication is two-way. The axis that goes up vertically is self-love and connection with Source—the Twin

Ray. The horizontal axis is cooperation with others—giving love to and receiving love from them.

Many of us working with celestial teams are solo practitioners and choose not to be around others. It is important to spend time alone to stay connected with Spirit. Some people need more alone time than others. I find it easier to hold my vibration steady when I am only dealing with my energy field. My inner dialogue provides non-stop amusement, but there comes a point when I need fellowship with someone who has skin on them!

We are already connected in higher realms. When we meet in person or online with other celestial shamans, we not only see how our part fits into the bigger picture, we exchange codes that unite divine initiatives and strengthen/activate our spiritual gifts. In the higher energy field created in our gatherings, we can expand and experience a cosmic opening. Walk-ins and soul exchanges may take place. There is support for the process and integration.

Each of us is working on different segments and parts of the Earth ascension project in various dimensions. We are a collective energy, amplifying, magnifying, and creating a resonant field. It is beneficial to spend time with other people who can reinforce our positive vision for the New Earth. Interacting with one another helps us all see our part in the project more clearly.

Celestial shamans intuitively communicate through telepathy as well as audible frequencies with their team of technicians, ethereal surgeons, and DNA geneticists who work with the human body template. These off-planet beings are multiverse wisdom keepers who are here to help humanity ascend to a higher level of consciousness. They desire to bring forth a new world that is loving and community-centered in mutual service to the light and one another. As our celestial teams gather with us, much communication goes on between them. We gain new information as they exchange energy and codes with us. We also do planetary and multidimensional work when we come together as a collaborative. Everything is harmonized.

There is another really important reason to get together. It allows us to expand and merge our fields. Interacting with others nourishes us and it nurtures the field we all hold. There is no fear of being harmed for being different. We do not have to shut down like we do with others who cannot accept us or like us. In the gathering of our tribes, we can be wide open in our collaboration. We can fully express ourselves and listen to what others share. There is no need to contract our field or shut others down when there is no right or wrong way to be. It is empowering when you can love yourself for being who you are instead of feeling like you do not fit in.

We need one another, yes. But it is best to have our main association with those who can help us keep a positive outlook and hold the vision of the new level of consciousness that we are entering. Our tribe is not necessarily our biological family. Our new paradigm family is made up of those who can encourage us and not create more fear. We may or may or may not be able to meet with them in person. I am very thankful for the internet that makes it possible for us to find one another.

We anchor, activate, and expand love to one another and to the awakening human population. There are many people waking up right now and they desperately need our support. Through our conversations and interactions with people in daily life, we can share insight and positively influence them on their journey. When people first wake up they may feel imbalanced or out-of-body, confused, or like they are going insane. The energy is strong and unfamiliar to the body. As celestial shamans abide in the expanded still-point field, we can send a vibration of calmness to those who are just beginning to open to their personal enlightenment. A group of light language intercessors came together online in February 2020. We opened a portal of peace that you can tap into right now. Use your breath and intention to access those codes that are embedded in this book.

Many intercessors on that call had been getting the message that there is nothing left to heal or fix because there is nothing wrong. Yet, my mind has difficulty believing it when I look at the world around me. That is because physical matter (density) has not caught up with what has been created in the reality of higher dimensions. Whenever we want to manifest something, we begin by making our request known to the Universe. We speak it out, put it in the vibratory field, or send it up as a prayer. We believe it is done, so we go about our lives and wait for it to manifest. We take intuitively guided steps or inspired action toward materialization, if necessary.

During my coaching sessions I use English to converse on a human level. However, most of the energy and codes come through my voice as I channel sounds and multiple bandwidths of light. Similar to a radio tuner, we are dialing into different "stations" to work with genetic codes, cosmic frequencies, electromagnetic fields, and frequency bands. Many times, celestial shamans travel inner-dimensionally into the underworld or into programs that are malfunctioning. We are cleaning viruses and correcting things that are out of alignment with love and integrity.

My friend Jacque told me that she has found herself in an incredibly humbling status of daily light language usage. When she takes a bath, light language flows through her in profoundly astonishing ways. Lately darker, denser energies are coming forth to be released for the collective. She says light language is the most efficient tool she has found.

Light language is a form of vibrational healing or sound channeling of the vector wave. Cosmic Source energy comes through our hands, voice, eyes, body movements, or hand mudras. The language or dialect that comes through is like a bandwidth that focuses a particular frequency toward the client's needs at that moment. I use the term "client" loosely, realizing that not all celestial shamans work with paying clients. You may be sending codes to friends, family members, a stranger on the street, to a community, or to the world at large. Our gatherings provide a platform to share our modalities and successes while asking questions and finding conformation that encourages us to continue our path.

Gifts from Other Lifetimes

The vast majority of us have had many incarnations on Earth before now. Some have been more favorable lifetimes than others. We are merging consciousnesses and multidimensional aspects and are bringing in the gifts, skills, and talents from other lifetimes. Perhaps these talents went underground because it was not safe for them to be used in another time period. Some people were killed in past lives for using magic or healing gifts. The energy on Earth is now allowing us to pick up tools and gifts we used previously and bring them forward to this lifetime.

I have found myself and other clients going all the way back to ancient Egypt, Atlantis, and Lemuria and accessing codes we deposited then in anticipation of the world becoming ready for those codes. Before Lemuria fell, we encoded things into caves, temples, and the air waves. We are now bringing the codes back online. We are transmitting them everywhere we go to help create the new world.

As you allow Source energy to flow through you, it is possible to speak languages of the guides of the person you are working with. Other times, one of your guides may speak or to beam a frequency that the client can plug into energetically. Sometimes the guides of the celestial shaman and the client have a conversation in light language as they discuss options for best outcomes. You can be a flowing channel for codes to meet the task at hand wherever you or others are in this journey.

There is no need to tell the codes what to do. They are instructions that align patterns according to the divine plan that seeks the highest and best for all. I do hear, feel, and see things that let me know where the energy is working. That is not to say you cannot direct the codes or know what they are doing. As you continue to grow in your spiritual abilities, you will instinctively understand and interpret more and more at a heart level. For now, light language and the written codes are here to bring us back to our senses— literally! We must learn to sense and trust our feelings, emotions, intuition, and heart more fully.

We are incorporating even more intergalactic vibrations and languages right now. Many celestial shamans are speaking a mixture of human languages and cosmic sounds as a way of expressing and integrating multidimensional beings in the human body. In doing so, we are allowing ourselves to become more comfortable with whatever vibration comes through. We do not fear that something evil will enter. We trust that nothing happens outside of divine will. That said, we will have our favorite vibrations that we work with more frequently.

There are frequencies in my voice that I have never had before. Some sound out of this world or like electronic pulses. Intuitive chanting may sound like Native American or aboriginal languages. Animal sounds come through as well. What have you been experiencing? Is there anything you have been holding back due to fear of rejection or feeling that it was not "normal" (whatever that is!)? It may seem quite weird to allow strange sounds to come through in your multidimensional channeling. Surrendering to Spirit helps move resistance out of the way, which will bring through different languages or vibrations that you may not normally work with. Take a moment now to open up and allow those sounds to come out. You are opening to new frequency bands.

Think of expanding your antenna bigger or further out so you are getting more cosmic signals. Begin to recognize and interact with the whole dial or spectrum of vibrations in all the languages. You will find that you can telepathically communicate with anybody, no matter what vibration they are emitting. You recognize that everyone has a personality that covers their true identity. When interacting with others, see them on a soul level and respond without ego. We may not always know exactly what our light language is doing or activating. If I am shaking my head "yes" when you speak unknown (to me) languages, it is because I can feel what you are saying. I do not have to understand or process the information in English.

As mentioned earlier, in our entertainment world, we have actors who play villains and actors who play heroes, but that is not who they really are. They have put aside their daily life and separated their personality from the character they are playing. Every human plays a role(s) in this movie we call life. Some "characters" are detestable and undesirable.

Sometimes we are the mirror to ugly energies and emotions. If you are mirroring something back at itself you are cancelling it out. This is why I do not worry about wearing or not wearing a mask in public. I prefer not to cover my face, but I can use my intention to change the vibration of anything. Consciously playing with emotional energy allows us to end the cycle of projecting. I do not imagine many of us want to be the mirror—especially if we do not realize we are being the mirror. If we do not recognize we are projecting, we (and others) may think we are being a bitch. If we are working on a conscious level with the higher mind, we know that we are clearing pockets of karma. It may not make you very popular in the meantime. We have to let go of wanting to be liked by everyone when we are pulling up the dredges and remnants of stuff that needs to be transmuted or integrated.

If you feel like you are playing the role of the bad guy (perhaps setting tough boundaries), try to see it from the perspective that you are doing it for the good of all—not to intentionally be mean. If you have an angry outburst or get frustrated, you may not understand why this happens. Try to look beyond the physical and see who you truly are in your Spirit. Self-forgiveness is valuable in this role-playing scenario. Many spirit beings walk with us as guides or guardians. They see us as we are, beyond fault or shadow. They always see our light. That is our role as well—to see light in every being including ourselves. Seeing with Spirit, or beyond what appears to be real, can heal all of us.

The human experience is meant to incorporate light and embody our divine true nature into the physical form while faced with challenges and opposition. This process of being human with divine awareness means we get to experience and embrace darkness in order to watch it vanish. Darkness and the unknown are frightening to a human. Yet, darkness is also beautiful because it offers us a chance to see ourselves and others for who they truly are aside from the roles we are playing. If we can shine the holy ray of compassion upon the behaviors and habits that we cannot stand about ourselves and others, then we will be ready to embrace beings who are too frightening for us right now.

Some disincarnate souls that we have trouble with or entities that we call attachments may not know that they are performing a role. Maybe it is not what they really want to be doing. Although many souls are not at that level of awareness, some get trapped in the role after the movie is over. They do not remember themselves as part of the God energy. In setting captives free and delivering them from "evil," we need to have compassion. We have all felt lost at some point. To feel separated from Source love and light is a lonely trap that feels like hell.

The construct of demons was created by humans who have kept parts of their own consciousness imprisoned or hidden. Most people believe in polar opposite forces: light and dark, good and evil, male and female, yin and yang, etc. This vast field of polarity allows consciousness to manifest in any way possible. Quantum physics explain this through vibration, frequency, and color spectrum. Light particles contained in a frequency can be measured. A "lighter" or "higher" frequency moves faster and contains more information than a "darker" frequency which contains more density. Neither is superior or inferior to the other. They are expressions of duality.

It is our judgment of these forces that has condemned the shadow and caused it to be repressed and shunned. Anything that is kept under pressure can eventually erupt. Is it any wonder that our individual and collective demons are coming out in full force as the light increases on our planet?

As we are incorporating parts of ourselves and reclaiming the full expression of the collective, we are not as bothered by malevolent energies. They are like an aggravating fly buzzing around. We are aware of the pesky beings, but rather than chasing them away or swatting at them, we learn to coexist. For the most part, there is mutual respect. I leave them alone and they leave me alone. If I do get stung or "tagged" by some denser force, I immediately feel it and take action to comfort my body and tend to my energetic needs. The only way an unpleasant force can get to you is if you lower your frequency to match theirs. Gratitude and laughter raise the vibration. Many times, I have the opportunity to send these beings into the light where they remember their own divinity.

Some of these so-called "fallen angels" have identified with matter so much, they have forgotten that they are Spirit. They have personified into a human body and become trapped in density. They cannot see their way clear. I sense that some are ready to be reintegrated into the light. They are free to ascend, but they are traumatized or paralyzed by their experience on the Earth plane. Like a bird in a cage with the door open, they remain in the role and do not fly to their accessible freedom.

If we fervently attend to retraining our personality, we will become more aware of our connection to one another and our relationship with Source. Thus, our social experiences and our respect for Mother Earth will improve. Captives will be set free!

CHAPTER 13 ~ Keeping a High Vibration

The world is moving through stressful times that feel like an initiation or trial run to see how ready we are to let go of fear and live in a new paradigm. As the old paradigm is passing away, we are urged to realize that we have incredible access to infinite power and creative possibility. It is common to feel uneasy or vulnerable as we shift from one state of being to another. Some days we are tapped into the infinite possibility of your future and everything looks bright. You feel invincible. Other days you may feel like you are hanging on to a scrap of faith just to get through. Consider these times we are now facing as a global rite of passage—the beginning of a much-needed restructuring of global power. More than ever, this is a time for keen discernment and to realize that we are powerful creators.

Corona means "crown" in Latin. The crown is the 7th chakra, our opening to higher consciousness. When a baby is born headfirst, the moment the head is first seen is called the "crowning." We are in the labor stages as we are being birthed into a new paradigm. A virus is a detrimental piece of code that copies itself and can corrupt a system or destroy data. The coronavirus is doing exactly what Source intended it to do—dismantling old systems that do not support the ascension of humanity. It is purging a web of distorted information in the human DNA and consciousness on Earth. Rather than addressing it with fear, see it as a component of shifting what is not beneficial. It offers all of us a chance to unplug and reboot as anomalies and malware are being removed from human programming. We are able to process energies and integrate frequencies that our bodies were not able to handle before. We are no longer just about talking about the ascension—we are actually embodying our higher self—part of Source that is unique and whole!

> "And the people stayed home. And read books, and listened, and rested, and exercised, and made art, and played games, and learned new ways of being, and were still. And listened more deeply. Some meditated, some prayed, some danced. Some met their shadows. And the people began to think differently. And the people healed. And in the absence of people living in ignorant, dangerous, mindless, and heartless ways, the Earth began to heal. And when the danger passed, and the people joined together again, they grieve their losses, and made new choices, and dreams new images, and created new ways to live and heal the Earth fully, as they have been healed."
>
> ~ Kitty O'Meara

It is tempting to follow the ideas and beliefs of others or look outside ourselves for comfort and answers. We have seen conflicting information in the media that keeps people living in fear. As aspects of Divine Source, we were not designed to live in fear. We are called to be in loving and respectful community with one another. How do you shine the light and hold a steady field of peace when people around you are panicking? The key is to be willing to trust that everything is happening for a reason rather than being resistant to the work that is being done in all of us. There is no judgment in the Christ Consciousness and the new era we are entering. Therefore, you are not being judged by your ability to hold a perfect vibration.

Your vibration is based upon your how willing you are to change, grow, and trust Source. Living in the moment and being connected with our body and personal energy field is not a pass or fail test. It is a daily decision to know yourself intimately. Since the ascension experience is about transformation through receiving an influx of higher vibrational energy, it can take a while for the energy to integrate. It depends upon how willing the recipient is to allow a shifting of the programmed personality. The more resistance we put up, the more our path will reflect hardship. And it may take longer to transverse the gap between where we are and where we truly want to be. Our fear of emotional vulnerability and hesitancy to explore the patterns created by the shadow side of our personality can prohibit this beautiful transformation.

> "During your transformation, you might feel like everything is falling apart, but in reality everything is coming together for your highest good. You are being pushed to evolve and get out of your comfort zone so you can live and experience your true greatness. Welcome change."
>
> ~ i.am.pranita on Instagram

The process of Homecoming can feel painful and intense as it deletes old programs. We need to gently support ourselves through this process. Listen to your body and practice intuitive self-care. If something does not feel right or is causing you pain, stop and reset. Sit with the energy and decide if the task is something you should continue and push through, or if this your time to relax and allow for integration. Come back to your own knowing, rather than looking to someone else for your truth.

When we allow ourselves to sit silently or to take a nap or engage in a creative process, it helps bring in codes needed for integrating pieces of our multidimensional self. If you are integrating in a higher aspect of yourself, your body may not know what to do with that level of energy. If the body is vibrating in a denser level it may not match the new codes. Ask for codes to be sent to the physical cells of your body to reprogram it and raise its vibration to be compatible with the new frequencies.

"Each step of the journey is made by following the heart instead of following the crowd and by choosing knowledge over the veils of ignorance."

~ Henri Bergson

Maintaining your personal 18 inches rather than tampering with someone else's will free you from judging others and help you to love yourself more. It is hard to allow someone we love to suffer or have a difficult experience. There are times when nothing we do or say is going to help someone who is resisting change. We may have to step back from the situation or person(s) and take care of our own needs and re-anchor our faith. We may need to ponder whether or not to continue a relationship that is draining or distracting us. Make decisions based upon how you feel Spirit is leading you.

Exposing our dark side is part of the process of becoming authentic. Whatever shows up in the world is a mirror reflecting what is going on in the collective field. Your reality does not have to match that image. Celestial shamans are way-showers. Decide what you want in your world and hold that vision steady. We are the light. The discordant forces we battle inside ourselves are showing us what has been. We do not have to engage in that war.

When you come to a place of neutrality, you can easily access the wise guidance in your heart space or still-point. This is where information and inspired instructions are available. It is the place of being and feeling, not doing. It is the "now moment" everyone speaks about but very few find as a life path.

Love is the medicine that heals all lack, darkness, sickness, and grievances. Wars and fighting will never lead us to love and accept ourselves and others without condition. We have choice in how we respond to each thought or emotion that arises.

Remember to . . .

- Be creative
- Be playful
- Stay present
- Feel your own energy
- Acknowledge your feelings
- Sing, tone, and speak light language
- Make music, listen to uplifting music
- Practice RBQT-18"™
- Be around others who can hold a peaceful field
- Avoid distractions
- Have a loving and patient relationship with yourself

- Comfort your inner child
- Love yourself unconditionally
- Live from a higher perspective
- Hold a space for new creation

Celestial shamans desire to embody Spirit within matter and transcend (elevate their consciousness or level of sentience) and rise above the heavy densities of the Earth plane. When faced with a situation that has the capability to pull you off course, remember to reset and be fully present in your body. When you are not carrying the weight of the past or living somewhere in the future it will be easier to live in the present moment where your purest vibration is resonating and broadcasting. You will be aware of anything that is asking to be resolved and integrated; you will meet that aspect of yourself with love.

A celestial shaman does not need to carry a tool bag. As a clear and pure channel for Source love and light, we are the tools. If there is some object or tool that we like, or some teaching we can borrow from other cultures, we can employ that, but we are not limited by rules or tradition. All the gifts and power are within us. It comes from the flow of energy connected with higher realms. You are anchoring codes, healing people, and crossing souls over without even having to try. Your work is becoming easier, faster, and it has less drama. As the divine feminine aspect comes into a harmonious position with the divine masculine, you will carry a peacefulness that people can feel. Share what you have learned in this book and help others create happiness within. Keep shining your light and sending ripples through the collective.

This is a new day, a new dimension, a new revelation allowing us to walk into a better way of being and living and relating. Let light and love spring forth in the hearts and minds of all. Try to relax into the flow of life—even allowing the painful things to be noticed. Speak gently to the fear or tension in your body every time it comes up. Focus on being kind to your inner child and on loving yourself and others more than you ever have.

The more we recognize the different parts we play, the less we judge ourselves. It takes away stress and pressure to know that you do not to have it all together all the time. One day you are playing one role. Another day you are playing a different part. Some days you are jumping through portals and timelines. Some days you may feel like you missed your cue. Some days you get to just be a human. Some days you roar with the power of God within you! Become the witness of the vibration from which you are making decisions. Choose nothing out of guilt, obligation, fear, or lack.

A movie is not filmed in one day. Various scenes are set up and the necessary characters are present. You may not know how everything is going to fit into the big picture, but you trust divine will. Things may not show up in chronological order, but the dots are being connected. The movie of Earth's ascension is in an editing stage right now. That is why we can sense that the work is already done, and yet is still being done. Once all the scenes are filmed and assembled, the movie will run seamlessly, and we will see things from a higher perspective. The curtain will soon open and all that we have been doing behind the scenes will be revealed.

Timelines are collapsing and there are multiple endings to the movie. We are expecting the outcome for the highest trajectory. There are outtakes from the old paradigm that will not make the final cut—old archetypes may not be present in a higher dimensional setting. We become more integrated and whole as we accept and love the roles that our shadow parts play. There is no need to fight or banish them. The despised "demons" and unacceptable parts of our human experience will transition to a new vibration. We begin to recognize all our experiences are part of the divine plan playing out in this movie or video game we call life. I encourage you to view life through the eyes of Spirit. Together, we are the producers, scriptwriters, characters, set builders, editors, and the wardrobe department supporting of our individual and collective realities. No need to get bogged down by worrying if your costume looks right or if you did a good job on the role you were playing. We are remembering our true selves and integrating all the roles we have played. We get to choose who we want to be next and what role we want to play from the best parts of our experiences. We will step into the new scene when all is ready.

There were times when I could not go to the next step until the cosmic technicians had cleared anomalies that they had interjected in the collective human form—or my particular body. We cannot jump ahead of divine perfection. If you are in a holding pattern and do not know what to do next, just BE! Work with the tri-vector concept while in this preparatory phase. We have a massive opportunity to reframe the density that is coming up to be healed. There is no better time to do our inner work and enter a new plane of existence. Use this time to transmute separation and see how magnificent you already are. If you need support in leaving the old ways and making room for the abundance awaiting you, please consider a coaching session with me. I would love to support you in identifying how you can carry your light more consistently.

It is time for people in all demographics to learn how to navigate through vibrational movement rather than thought movement. We begin by working with our own three-part integration process, then we branch into small core groups where we practice creating a resonate group field. From there, individuals who are able to feel the vibrational field inside and outside the body can take this technique into their practice and teach others how to unify Spirit, body, and personality. When we engage the full sensory ability of the body, we have lasting results rather than using thought to rehash old trauma and stories. Everyone has access to this technique because it is within us. Once we start meeting and sharing, we will begin to translate the similarities and make practical application. Brenda Williams and I have some exciting ways that we want to interact and share with you. Check the events page on my website https://weare1inspirit.com to stay informed of opportunities to join us online.

"I invite you to return to the innocence and curiosity of a child experiencing something for the first time. Allow your imagination to take you to a new level of awareness. The experiential format provides an opportunity to recognize and remember the electromagnetic field of vibrational movement that is both internal and external. This opens an opportunity to experience how you move within the greater field of experience. The navigation into our personal and collective experience, in resonance with our higher awareness and knowing becomes a natural and organic process of our moment-to-moment experience...as it was in the Beginning."

~ Brenda Julian Williams, A Wholistic Concept

The tri-system work is a challenge, but it is also fun. I have never been as carefree and happy as I am now. Loving myself unconditionally allows me to laugh with/at myself and have interesting dialogues with the inner voices that offer me prankish options that I quickly decline.

> "One day when you wake up you will find that you have become a forest. You have grown roots and found strength in them that no one thought you had. You have become stronger and more beautiful full of life-giving qualities. You have learned to take all the negativity around you and turn it into oxygen for easy breathing. Wild creatures live inside, and beautiful birds rest inside your mind and you call them memories. You have become an incredible self-sustaining thing of epic proportions. And you should be proud of yourself of how far you have come from the seeds of who you used to be."

~ Nikita Gill, You Have Become a Forest

We are embodying more Spirit as our personality is challenged with changes that cause us to focus on what is really important. The still-point that we access can launch a whole new concept into the world. It is the concept of the origin. It is how we began, and it is how we come Home. Keep trusting that divine will is orchestrating this entire scenario. Egoic personalities do not have control of what is happening. There is no battle except the one we wage within our own mind. Do not worry about what anyone thinks of you. Appreciate your body, regardless of its appearance, shape, size, color, etc. Love the personality that allows Source to experience various levels of density in human form. We are entering unity consciousness! Are you ready to open to something grander? Are you ready to see where life is leading you?

Your guides are you in holographic shards that represents your unique expression of God. You are me. I am you. We are One. We can do this! We can embody the 6th element!

BIBLIOGRAPHY

"Leticia's Walk-in Follow-up Quote." Email correspondence. 15 June 2020.

"Nikola Tesla - Limitless Energy & the Pyramids of Egypt". After Skool. <https://www.youtube.com/watch?v=Ft1waA3p2_w>.

"Shadow Work is Healthy." hbbbiofeedback quote on Instagram, 13 March 2020.

"Vortex Math Part 1 and 2 Nikola Tesla 3 6 9 The Key to the Universe." Know-how. <https://www.youtube.com/watch?v=OXbVZc10Ink>.

1 Kings 17:7-16 New International Version. Bible Gateway.com. <https://www.biblegateway.com/passage/?search=1+Kings+17%3A+7-16&version=NIV>.

1 Thessalonians 4:16-18. King James Version of the Bible. Accessed 14 June 2020 <https://www.biblegateway.com/passage/?search=1%20Thessalonians%204:16-18;&version=KJV>

Anatamata, Doe. Intuition quote. Accessed 24 March 2020. <https://healingbrave.com/blogs/all/quotes-listen-to-your-heart>.

Aragon, Britta. Founder, Detox Your Life, Inc. Email correspondence. 11 April 2020

Balasubramaniam, Bairavee. Quote posted on Facebook. Accessed <https://www.facebook.com/bairavee.balasubramaniam?fref=nf>

Bequer, Azrya Cohen. "What Psychedelics Told Me About the Coronavirus." <https://medium.com/@azrya/what-psychedelics-told-me-about-the-coronavirus-730a4a6b9714>.

Bergson, Henri. AZ Quotes. Accessed 25 March 2020. <https://www.azquotes.com/quote/515117>.

Braden, Gregg. "The Ancient Technique to Making Tough Decisions". Paraphrased. <<https://youtu.be/exHp3L_c2Lg>.

Carey, Kenneth X. The Starseed Transmissions. 1995, HarperCollins.

Carroll, Amy. "Birthing starseeds before integrating full aspect of Divine Mother/Father". Email correspondence. 5 March 2020.

Kahn, Matt. Quote on his Facebook page. 8 April 2020.

King James Version of the Bible. Isaiah 61:1. Accessed 20 May 2020. <https://www.biblegateway.com/passage/?search=Isaiah+61%3A1&version=KJV>.

King James Version of the Bible. Acts 1: 9-11. Accessed 14 June 2020. <https://www.biblegateway.com/passage/?search=Acts+1%3A+9-11&version=KJV>.

Kryon through Lee Carroll. "The You in the Mirror" on Instagram, posted by Urban.sharman.3 Accessed 10 March 2020.

Matthew 18:2-4 New International Version of the Bible. Accessed 10 May 2020. <https://www.biblegateway.com/passage/?search=Matthew+18%3A2-4&version=NIV>.

Matthew 6:9 New International Version of the Bible. Accessed 1 May 2020. <https://www.biblegateway.com/passage/?search=Matthew+6%3A9&version=NIV>.

Meacham, William. "The Quantum Level of Reality." 2008. <http://www.bmeacham.com/whatswhat/Quantum.html#2.Quantum%20Physics|outline>.

New Century Bible. John 3:1-8. Accessed 18 May 2020. <https://www.biblegateway.com/passage/?search=John+3%3A1-8&version=NCV>.

New International Version Bible. Genesis 50:20. Accessed 18 May 2020. <https://biblehub.com/genesis/50-20.htm>

O'Meara, Kitty. Accessed 24 March 2020 on Facebook. Author credits found at <https://womenyoushouldknow.net/fact-people-stayed-home-viral-poem-kitty-omeara-2020/>.

Philippians 2:6-7. Common English Bible. Accessed 18 May 2020. <https://www.biblegateway.com/passage/?search=Philippians+2%3A6-7&version=CEB>.

Price, Jamye. "Freedom Present, Past Released" <https://jamyeprice.com/releasing-the-past/>.

Price, Jamye. October 2015 Light Blast Newsletter. Email correspondance.

Quan Yin, Amorah. "The Pleiadian Workbook: Awakening Your Divine Ka." 1995 Bear & Company.

Sarmiento, Ulla. "How Does Reincarnation Work?" <http://bigpicturequestions.com/how-does-reincarnation-work/>. Accessed 22 April 2020.

Seppi, Sheila. Email correspondence. 30 March 2020.

Sharp, Randy and Lowery, Donny R. "Why Does it Have to Be (Wrong or Right)." LyricFind. Accessed 14 April 2020. <https://www.songfacts.com/lyrics/restless-heart/why-does-it-have-to-be-wrong-or-right>.

Torroni, Amanda. Hippie Peace Freaks on Facebook. Accessed 26 March 2020. <https://www.facebook.com/TheHippiePeaceFreaks/>.

Williams, Brenda Julian. The Tri-Vector SYSTEM™ which consists of The Triad Wave Sequencing, RBQT-18", and The Wholistic Concept (Spirit/Body/Personality). Accessed 19 June 2020. <https://conversationsofadifferentkind.com/>

ABOUT YVONNE

As a celestial shaman with several walk-in experiences, Yvonne Perry helps people integrate multidimensional soul aspects. She is a practitioner of light codes, offering one-on-one coaching to help people manage energy, access and anchor vibrations of higher realms, and live authentically.

Holding a Bachelor of Science in Metaphysics from the American Institute for Holistic Theology, she understands the "Homecoming" or ascension process. In her speaking engagements and online workshops, Yvonne activates people into the expression of light language.

For more information, please see https://weare1inspirit.com.

Other books written by Yvonne Perry

- Light Language Emerging ~ Activating Ascension Codes & Integrating Body, Soul, & Spirit.
- Walk-ins Among Us ~ Open Your Personal Portal to Cosmic Awareness
- Shifting into Purer Consciousness ~ Integrating Spiritual Transformation with the Human Experience
- Whose Stuff Is This? ~ Finding Freedom from the Thoughts, Feelings, and Energy of Those Around You
- More Than Meets the Eye ~ True Stories about Death, Dying and Afterlife
- The Sid Series ~ A Collection of Holistic Stories for Children

Made in the USA
Columbia, SC
10 June 2024

36922633R00124